SECOND EDITION

C1 HIGHER
SUCCESS WITH
BUSINESS

SUCCESS WITH BUSINESS resources (including audio and
answer sheets for the practice exam)

http://www.eltexampreparation.com/success/success-business

Password: succ!BUS#2

NATIONAL
GEOGRAPHIC
L E A R N I N G

Australia · Brazil · Mexico · Singapore · United Kingdom · United States

National Geographic Learning,
a Cengage Company

Success with Business Higher Workbook
2nd Edition
Paul Dummett, Colin Benn

Publisher: Sharon Jervis

Project Manager: Hattie Fell

Editorial Manager: Claire Merchant

Head of Strategic Marketing ELT: Charlotte Ellis

Product Marketing Manager ELT: Victoria Taylor

Head of Production and Design: Celia Jones

Senior Content Project Manager: Sue Povey

Manufacturing Manager: Eyvett Davis

Composition: emc design ltd

Cover Design: emc design ltd

Audio Producer: James Richardson

For permission to use material from this text or product,
submit all requests online at **www.cengage.com/permissions**

Further permissions questions can be emailed to
permissionrequest@cengage.com

ISBN: 978-1-4737-7249-6

National Geographic Learning
Cheriton House, North Way
Andover, Hampshire, SP10 5BE
United Kingdom

Locate your local office at **international.cengage.com/region**

Visit National Geographic Learning online at **ELTNGL.com**
Visit our corporate website at **www.cengage.com**

Acknowledgements

The publishers would like to dedicate the Success with Business series to the memory of its inspirational editor, David Riley.

The publishers would like to thank and acknowledge the following sources:

Text
page 5: Source: Honda Sochiro; **page 26**: Source: Data sourced from The World Factbook 2017 from the Central Intelligence Agency; **page 28**: Source: Eight winning tips to make your financial plan profitable - Based on article Don't wait for tax time to look at the bottom line by C.J.Hayden; **page 55**: Source: Hillary Clinton; Source: Donald Trump; **page 60**: Source: Robert Reich; Source: Jimmy Carter; Source: William Greider; Source: Robert J Samuelson; Source: Jack Welch; Source: Fredric Jameson; Source: John Sweeney; **page 62**: Source: The Dos and Taboos of Body Language by Roger Axtell - reproduced with permission of John Wiley and Sons Inc.

Cover Image
Luxy Images Limited/Alamy Stock Photo

Photos
5 © Takeyoshi Tanuma/Contributor/The LIFE Picture Collection/Getty Images; **11** © monkeybusinessimages/iStock/Thinkstock; **17** © Rawpixel/iStock/Thinkstock; **20** © monkeybusinessimages/iStock/Thinkstock; **25** © antpkr/iStock/Thinkstock; **32** © fizkes/iStock/Thinkstock; **35** © targovcom/iStock/Thinkstock; **40** © Anna_Om/iStock/Thinkstock; **42** © hjalmeida/iStock/Thinkstock; **45** © holub3dmax/iStock/Thinkstock; **50** © IakovKalinin/iStock/Thinkstock; **55** © NurPhoto/Contributor/NurPhoto/Getty Images; **57** © Highwaystarz-Photography/iStock; **62** © stevecoleimages/iStock/Thinkstock.

Printed in the United Kingdom by Ashford Colour Press
Print Number: 01   Print Year: 2019

CONTENTS

1.1   Working life

Describing working life

1 Put the correct word into each gap (1–11) to complete this biography of Soichiro Honda, the founder of the Honda Motor™ Company.

> set up   ~~founded~~   worked   joined   retired
> moved   left   recruited   graduated
> trained   educated   applied

Soichiro Honda, the man who (**0**) *founded* the Honda Motor Company, has often been described as a maverick in a nation of conformists. He was born in 1906 and was

(**1**) _____ only to elementary level. When he became a teenager, he (**2**) _____ home to find his fortune in Tokyo. In 1922, he (**3**) _____ for a job in an auto-repair shop where they (**4**) _____ him to be an auto-mechanic. Honda had such a passion for cars that he devoted his spare time to building his own racing car out of handmade parts and an old aircraft engine.

By 1937, Honda had (**5**) _____ his own company to make piston rings. However, he soon realised that he lacked the knowledge to do this well, so he (**6**) _____ a technical school. However, he never formally (**7**) _____ from the school because he did not bother to take the final examination. According to Honda, the certificate was worth less than the price of a movie ticket. What he treasured was the knowledge that he learnt from the school and which he could apply in his own factory.

In 1948, Honda Motor Company began manufacturing small motorcycles. These were dismissed by the dominant American and British manufacturers of the time, but in reality, the inexpensive vehicles brought new people to motorcycling and changed the industry forever. 'Honda has always (**8**) _____ ahead of the times and I attribute its success to the fact that the firm possesses dreams and youthfulness,' said Soichiro Honda.

An inventor at heart, Soichiro Honda often (**9**) _____ alongside his employees, researching and developing new automobile technology. In 1959, he (**10**) _____ Takeo Fujisawa, a business executive, to manage the company so that Honda could concentrate on the engineering work. In 1973, Honda (**11**) _____ on the company's 25th anniversary.

2 Put each word in the correct form to complete the sentence.

0 Students wishing to be considered for a grant must fill out the D17 *application* form.   APPLY

1 I was extremely lucky to find a job; the _____ rate in our area is about 20%.   EMPLOY

2 We got a lot of attention: on the course I attended there were only two _____ to every one trainer.   TRAIN

3 Our _____ policy doesn't allow us to employ people without a university degree.   RECRUIT

4 I'm much more interested in job satisfaction than the level of my _____ .   PAY

5 I've just got a _____ to department manager, but in fact my responsibilities are the same as before.   PROMOTE

6 We received over 500 _____ for just 15 vacancies.   APPLY

7 She's not very happy in her _____ ; she'd prefer to be working still.   RETIRE

8 I'll be out of the office all next week; I'm on a sales _____ course.   TRAIN

Gerund and infinitive

3 Group the words and phrases with a similar meaning.

> I plan   There's no point   I am prepared
> It's useless   I am considering   I adore
> I'm keen on   I am thinking of   I wasn't able
> I aim   I am happy   I failed

1 a It's not worth
   b _____ } + gerund
   c _____

2 a I intend
   b _____ } + infinitive
   c _____

3 a I am thinking about
   b _____ } + gerund
   c _____

4 a I am willing
   b _____ } + infinitive
   c _____

5 a I enjoy
   b _____ } + gerund
   c _____

6 a I didn't manage
   b _____ } + infinitive
   c _____

4 Rewrite each sentence using a gerund or infinitive phrase.

0 Peter thinks golf is a great way to relax.
   Peter enjoys *playing golf*.

1 It's very strange for me to drive on the left.
   I'm not used to _____ .

2 Her main strength is management of people.
   She is good at _____ .

3 I am definitely going to leave at the end of the year.
   I plan _____ .

4 Did you have any luck contacting Jane?
   Did you manage _____ ?

5 She thinks that increasing the prices is a mistake.
   She is reluctant _____ .

6 Were there any problems with the software download?
   Did you have any difficulty _____ ?

7 Will I have to speak in French?
   Does the job involve _____ ?

8 Can you tell me your approximate time of arrival?
   When do you expect _____ ?

9 We could go to the cinema tonight, if you like?
   What do you think about _____ ?

10 Don't call me between 10 and 12.
   Please avoid _____ .

11 The flights are all full. How about the train?
   The flights are full. Would you consider _____ ?

12 I don't need to fly business class on such a short journey.
   It's not worth _____ .

Pronunciation

5 Look at where stress falls in the following words. What rules can you make?

reti**re**   dism**iss**   **bu**siness   **know**ledge   **pros**pects
empl**oy**   recr**uit**   **off**ice   **for**tune   ap**ply**

6 Mark where the stress falls in each of these words.

background   supply   contract   student   promote
involve   retain   college   attend   status

7 Each of these words can be a noun OR a verb. Decide which each one is according to where the stress is marked.

pre**sent**   per**mit**   **ob**ject   **in**crease
conflict   **con**test   ex**port**   in**sult**

Reading

8 Which of these job advertisements:

0 is aimed at people fresh from university? A
1 requires the candidate to be self-motivated? ____
2 is part of an equal opportunities scheme? ____
3 asks for proof of the candidate's honesty and suitability? ____
4 demands a high level of qualifications? ____
5 doesn't require the candidate to have worked in that field before? ____
6 is to join a young, fast-growing company? ____
7 offers the chance of promotion? ____

A

Trainee consultants

We are looking for bright and capable young graduates to join our highly successful business consulting team. No direct experience is necessary as training will be given, but candidates must show an understanding of the business environment and a willingness to learn. Excellent career prospects. Apply in writing to PO Box 34.

B

Senior health co-ordinator

Lancashire Health Authority invites independent and responsible candidates with a master's degree in nursing, ten years' nursing experience and at least three years' management experience to apply for this challenging post. Lancashire Authority will consider each application on its own merits, regardless of the candidate's sex, religion or ethnic background.

C

Web designers

Sparking Solutions was voted 'most dynamic newcomer' by *IT World* magazine two years ago. Our reputation is built on our ability to provide innovative, creative and fun solutions in the world of online marketing. Sounds like you? Apply to gemma@brightandsparking.com Please supply character references.

1.2 Asking and answering questions

Indirect questions

1 Read the interview between a journalist and the chairman of an energy company, following a 15% rise in prices to its electricity customers. Put the sentences in the right order.

1 First of all, Dr Wolf, can you tell me why this price rise is necessary?

2 Obviously, it's not something we wanted to do. It has been forced on us by higher oil prices.

_____ I can't speak for others, but I would be surprised if they didn't increase them in the near future.

_____ And finally, do you know why other companies haven't increased their prices by the same amount?

_____ These new prices are necessary to protect our future profits, not our past profits.

_____ But you don't actually produce much of your electricity from burning oil, do you?

_____ But even if gas has gone up, how can you justify these prices when you have just announced record profits?

_____ Oh, I see. So you'll be making just as much money out of your customers this year, will you?

_____ In fact, our profits this year will be used to fund a very expensive investment programme in our network.

_____ No, but the price of gas is linked to the price of oil and we do burn a lot of gas.

2 Convert these questions into direct questions.

0 Can you tell me why this price rise is necessary?
Why is this price rise necessary?

1 But you don't actually produce much of your electricity from burning oil, do you?

_____

_____

2 So you'll be making just as much money out of your customers this year, will you?

_____

_____

3 Do you know why other companies haven't increased their prices by the same amount?

_____

_____

3 Put the words into the correct order to make questions.

0 how / far / is / you / know / do / the station
Do you know how far the station is?

1 quite / you / aren't / inexperienced / are / you

_____

_____ ?

2 sales experience / how / have / do / much / you

_____

_____ ?

3 you / think / you / for the job / have / do / the necessary skills

_____

_____ ?

4 you / have / haven't / done / you / before / this kind of work

_____

_____ ?

5 like / a coffee / you / would

_____

_____ ?

6 don't / in London / you / live / you / do

_____

_____ ?

7 why / leave / last job / you / your / did

_____

_____ ?

8 why / you / tell / me / you / this job / can / attractive / find

_____

_____ ?

1.3 Reading Test: Part One

The following article, taken from *Management Now* magazine, is about young people's attitudes to work. Give yourself about 12 minutes to do this reading test.

- Look at the sentences below and read the comments by five managers on the attitudes of young workers to their jobs.
- Match each statement (1–7) to one of the extracts (A, B, C, D or E).
- You will need to use some of the letters more than once.

0 The education system does not prepare young people for working life. D

1 It is the older generation who must accept that attitudes have changed. _____

2 Young people's free time is very important to them. _____

3 Young workers are just as dedicated to their jobs as in the past. _____

4 Young people are very concerned about their earning power. _____

5 Employers cannot assume their employees will stay with them for a long time. _____

6 Young people do not have the patience to train and learn at work. _____

7 It suits companies too, if employees come and go. _____

C

I think that the work-life balance that young people have found is much healthier than it was in the past. They don't just live for work – they think about what they are working for. At the same time employers have moved to take account of this by offering more flexibility in working hours, better maternity or paternity leave conditions so that young parents can have more time with their children, and so on. It's a natural evolution. Just because young people have more commitment to getting their home life right, it doesn't necessarily follow that they are less committed to their jobs.

A

I find that the priorities of young employees are very different to my generation and previous generations. Leisure time is now much more organised than it was 20 years ago. When my parents had a break from work they used to do very little other than just relax. Nowadays, people want to plan an activity holiday or an action-packed weekend – to go diving or climbing or whitewater rafting. So necessarily they spend more time thinking about and planning these leisure events. This naturally has a knock-on effect on their work – they think less about work and more about leisure time.

B

Young workers certainly feel less commitment to their employers than in the past. But in many ways employers have themselves to blame for this. The demands on companies to be more competitive means that they hire people and then lay them off pretty much as they please. They need this flexibility. In other words, they don't show much loyalty to their own staff. What we are seeing now is a reaction to this. Employees have much less loyalty to their employers these days. If you ask a young person how many jobs he expects to have in his life, he will generally say about five to ten.

D

I worry that standards in our schools and universities have dropped quite dramatically and that people entering the workforce are very poorly equipped to deal with the demands of working life. What is more worrying is that the graduates themselves don't realise this. They think they have all the necessary qualifications and knowledge to be successful at work, when in fact they are lacking. So when they are faced with the prospect of learning more on the job and serving their time to gain this necessary experience, they become frustrated. The fact is that many of them have an over-inflated opinion of their own worth to the company, and they need to be made aware of this.

E

The attitudes of young workers are part of the change in values that we see around us generally. The most significant of these values are: first, a fear of being poor. There are so many images of material wealth around and young people want a part of it. Second, the belief that respect has to be earned – it cannot just be expected by elders or seniors at work. Third, a belief in expressing yourself rather than controlling yourself, which perhaps earlier generations thought was a virtue. So we, the older generation, must accept that these are the values of today and adapt to them in order to get the best from our young workforce.

2.1 Growing the company

Parts of a company

1 Write the word that fits the definition. The first letter has been given.

0 A company which pays a fee to use another company's name and sell its services:
   a f ranchise

1 A building where finished goods or raw materials are stored: a w _____

2 A company which is more than 50% owned by another (holding or parent) company:
   a s _____

3 A building where manufacturing, assembling or packing activity takes place: a p _____

4 The offices where the top management and administration are based: the h _____

5 A (large) part of a company that has responsibility for one area or activity: a d _____

2 Complete each newspaper headline using a word or phrase from the box.

| expands   sell off   go public   goes bankrupt |
| merge   takeover   laid off |

British bank fears _____ by cash-rich Spanish giant

Car plant closes: 800 _____

Keltel to _____ failing Internet business

BP and Shell _____ to form world's largest oil company

3 Complete the table.

Verb	Noun
expand	expansion
develop	
merge	
acquire	
grow	
innovate	innovation
	solution
	classification
	evolution
	tendency

Pronunciation

4 Look at where the stress falls in the following words of three syllables or more. What rules can you make about: a) those ending in -*ion* b) the rest?

innováment   responsibílity   expánsion   téndency
prodúction   solútion   acquisítion   cómpany
révenue   actívity

5 Mark where the stress falls in each of these words.

bankruptcy   evolution   division   subsidiary
strategy   distribution   significant   competition
competitive   philosophy

Deanly shares will _____ next year

Administrators called in as Lanco _____

Chemico _____ its European operations by buying Toxico

Past tenses

6 Complete the table of irregular verbs.

Present	Past	Past participle
begin		begun
become	became	
lose	lost	
buy		
put		put
rise		risen
fall	fell	
feel		
spend	spent	
find		found
found		

7 Complete this extract from a newspaper article by choosing the best sentence (A–G) for each gap (1–6).

The extraordinary fact about many successful businesses in the UK is that in the last 20 years they have not made their money from what they produce or sell. (**0**) A Take the example of St Coates College. (**1**) _____ It targeted the children of rich Europeans who wanted to send their children to the UK to study for their pre-university qualification. (**2**) _____ Business was good, however, and in the mid-70s the college decided it made more sense to buy houses in the neighbourhood to use as accommodation. (**3**) _____ Over the next 15 years their value tripled. (**4**) _____ The profits of the business itself, after servicing the property loans, were, by comparison, only moderate. St Coates is not the only business to have made its money in this way. (**5**) _____ But what has been lost along the way? (**6**) _____ Now, meeting the demand for products and services is no longer of the same interest – all a person needs to do is buy a property and sit on it for ten years.

A Rather they have profited from huge rises in the value of property.

B By the early 1990s it had purchased more than 20 such properties.

C It was founded in the 1960s as a college for the International Baccalaureate Exam.

D Twenty years ago, before the property boom, people were making things and providing services.

E The same model has been applied in many sectors and places all over the country.

F During its early years it used to rent accommodation to house these students.

G So the assets of the college increased enormously.

8 Some of the following extracts from a transport company's annual report contain mistakes with tenses. If the sentence is correct, mark it with a ✓. If it is wrong, correct it.

0 2017 ~~has been~~ a better year than we had originally anticipated.   was

00 At the beginning of the year, we <u>won</u> a contract to build a new metro system in Singapore.   ✓

1 Even though revenue was down over the course of the year, our profit margins <u>improved</u>.   _____

2 In April, we <u>had begun</u> work on a bus terminal in Shanghai.   _____

3 In Shanghai we used the same design that we <u>used to use</u> in Beijing a year earlier.   _____

4 Because many existing projects <u>were coming</u> to an end, we made it a priority to look for new business.   _____

5 In May, a new head of International Business <u>has been</u> appointed.   _____

6 We found that we <u>wasted</u> a lot of time in the planning stages.   _____

7 The official opening <u>was</u> attended by the president of Iran.   _____

8 Our R & D department <u>was working</u> on a new high-speed railway which will be launched next year.   _____

Organisational culture

9 Write in the missing letters to complete the chart.

E _ _ l _ y _ _ s   Customers

          Stakeholders

_ h _ _ eh _ _ _ e _ s   S _ _ _ lie _ s

          Lo _ a _ com _ _ _ ity

10 Make each noun into an adjective to complete each statement.

0 I feel secure in my job.   SECURITY

1 I am very _____ in the development of new products.   INVOLVEMENT

2 Customers are generally very _____ with the service they get.   SATISFACTION

3 We have a very _____ structure, with about 15 levels from top to bottom.   HIERARCHY

4 It's a very _____ company which empowers individuals.   INNOVATION

5 I am consulted both on everyday matters and also on more _____ decisions.   STRATEGY

11 Make each adjective into a noun to complete each statement.

6 At Google™ the emphasis is on _____ .   INFORMAL

7 Like most banks, our culture is influenced by the amount of _____ .   BUREAUCRATIC

8 The most important thing for employees is to have _____ ; not constant change.   CONSISTENT

9 In advertising, the main thing is to bring out employees' natural _____ .   CREATIVE

10 _____ can be financial or simply a few words of praise.   RECOGNISED

12 Below is a checklist for a healthy work environment. Complete the statements by choosing the best word from the box.

satisfaction	recognised	~~values~~	clear
balance	mutual	retention	reward
empowered	welfare		

Healthy Workplace Checklist

☐ Senior leadership in my organisation **(0)** values employees (eg takes employees' needs into account when key decisions are being made).

☐ Workplace health is the responsibility of all leaders (senior leaders down to front-line supervisors) in my organisation.

☐ My organisation walks the talk when it comes to work-life **(1)** _____ . (eg we do not **(2)** _____ employees who work long hours, just those who are productive).

☐ Employees in my organisation feel **(3)** _____ : they have a great degree of control over how they do their work and are involved in decisions that affect them.

☐ I work in a safe environment where on-the-job accidents are very rare.

☐ Employees in my organisation feel that the work they do is **(4)** _____ and that they get adequate feedback.

☐ I work in a culture of **(5)** _____ trust and respect.

☐ Customer **(6)** _____ is high, but does not come at the expense of employee **(7)** _____ .

☐ There are **(8)** _____ lines of communication (both top-down and bottom-up) in my organisation.

☐ People enjoy coming to work and attendance is very high.

☐ My organisation enjoys high **(9)** _____ because people do not want to leave.

2.2 Presenting facts

1 Match each phrase on the left with the one closest in meaning on the right.

0 Let's get started	A Feel free to interrupt
1 It's worth noting	B That brings me to the end
2 the main points	C To sum up
3 Stop me at any time	D Shall we begin?
4 Can everyone hear alright?	E I should mention
5 I digress	F Getting back to the subject
6 In conclusion	G I won't take up much of your time
7 I'll finish there	H Would you like me to speak up?
8 I'll try to be brief	I the key issues

2 Complete this biography of Zhang Xin, one of China's leading entrepreneurs, by writing ONE word in each gap (1–10).

The life and career of Zhang Xin, a woman who, along (**0**) with her husband, founded one of China's leading real estate companies and who is now listed as one of the world's most powerful women, is a classic rags-to-riches story. Zhang was born in 1965 and brought up in a poor suburb of Beijing. (**1**) _____ an early age, she was determined to improve her situation. After the family moved to Hong Kong (**2**) _____ her teens, Zhang did 12-hour shifts at a local factory to save money for her education. When she was 19, she flew to London, where she studied at a secretarial college (**3**) _____ eventually winning grants and scholarships to study at other universities. She graduated from Cambridge with a master's degree in Development Economics in 1992.
She then applied (**4**) _____ a job at the multinational firm Goldman Sachs and was taken on (**5**) _____ their Hong Kong office. After Zhang and her husband, Pan Shiyi, married in 1994, she moved back (**6**) _____ Beijing and together they set up their own real estate development company: SOHO China.
Two decades later, SOHO's office developments were seen all (**7**) _____ Beijing and Shanghai.

Zhang Xin has employed many of the world's most famous architects, such as Zaha Hadid, to design SOHO buildings, and has won many awards (**8**) _____ her work. Although Zhang's personal wealth has been estimated to be well (**9**) _____ US$3 billion, she remains very modest. She dresses simply, drives a normal car and never flies first class. Realising the impact of her education on her life, she and her husband have (**10**) _____ worked together to establish a foundation to help poor people to become better educated.

3 This sentence is grammatically incorrect: 'I'd like to talk you about my experience.' Instead, we can either say 'I'd like to talk about …' or 'I'd like to talk to you about …' or 'I'd like to tell you about …'. Correct the following sentences.

0 I need to talk my manager about that.
talk _to_ my manager

1 I'd like to present you our latest design.

_____

2 I'm going to describe you the development over the last four years.

_____

3 And I'd like to ask to you this question: why …?

_____

4 Can anyone tell why we should take such a risk?

_____

5 When I have explained you the reasons, you will understand.

_____

6 The next graph shows to you how we achieved these results.

_____

4 Imagine you are going to discuss the points below. Write sentences to present your opinion. Use the phrases in the box on page 54 to help you.

- Do you think it's better to work for a big organisation or a small company?
- Do you think management of people is something that can be learnt, or is it a natural quality?
- What do you think will be the really big growth areas of the economy over the next 15 years?

2.3 Speaking Test: Part One

1 Complete the responses to the examiner's questions using the phrases in the box.

> ~~very much~~   actually   not really
> I doubt it   I don't see it that way   for me
> I agree   on the whole

0 *Do you like living in Beijing?*
Very much. It's a really exciting city.

1 *So, French is your first language?*
_____ , it's German.

2 *Is it a well-paid job?*
Yes but, _____ , money is not the most important thing.

3 *Outsourcing does have many advantages.*
_____ . I think it is a very risky strategy.

4 *I believe it's a very competitive sector.*
_____ , that's true, but there are opportunities.

5 *Would you like to work in the public sector?*
_____ . It tends to be less dynamic.

6 *And do you think you will stay in Singapore?*
_____ . It's only a two-year contract.

7 *Choosing the right course is very important.*
_____ . It affects your whole career.

2 What do these examiners' comments mean? Match each comment (1–5) with one of the phrases (A–F).

0 That sounds exciting. I expect you're raring to go.	A If you don't take risks, you won't win anything.
1 Well it's not everyone's cup of tea.	B Good luck.
2 You've obviously done your homework.	C You must be keen to start.
3 Nothing ventured, nothing gained.	D I approve of your decision.
4 Well, I wish you all the best.	E It doesn't suit everybody.
5 I think that's very wise.	F You've researched it carefully.

3 Each of the student's responses below contains two mistakes which are underlined. Correct them.

0 **Examiner** Where are you working at the moment?
Candidate I am working <u>like</u> an apprentice <u>on</u> a pharmaceutical company.
I am working as an apprentice for a …

1 **Examiner** What does your job involve exactly?
Candidate I am responsible <u>of</u> searching the press <u>all days</u> for articles about our company.

2 **Examiner** Will you continue to work there at the end of your apprenticeship?
Candidate Yes, I hope <u>it</u>. But maybe I <u>must</u> apply for a job with another company.

3 **Examiner** And what do you hope to be doing ten years from now?
Candidate My ambition is <u>that I will work</u> in the marketing field, because that is what I <u>am specialised</u> in.

4 **Examiner** Do you think it's OK for pharmaceutical companies to advertise medicines?
Candidate It depends <u>for</u> what kind of product they are advertising. In my <u>vision</u>, it's fine to advertise if you are honest about the benefits.

5 **Examiner** But perhaps that's not always the case?
Candidate I <u>am agree</u> with you that some companies overstate benefits, but <u>in whole</u> they are very responsible.

3.1 Communication at work

Business communication

1 Complete this job advertisement for an assistant press officer by writing the correct verb in each gap (1–9).

Assistant press officer wanted

We are seeking a motivated, independent press relations officer to assist our busy team. Candidates should have at least ten years' experience in the field, preferably with a multinational corporation. The job will involve (**0**) making and (**1**) _____ calls from members of the press; (**2**) _____ press releases; (**3**) _____ public meetings with the Chairman and, where necessary, (**4**) _____ the minutes; coaching the Chairman before he (**5**) _____ presentations or speeches; helping to (**6**) _____ the company's annual report; (**7**) _____ news about the company's activities on our website; liaising with the marketing department about the (**8**) _____ of advertising campaigns; keeping department heads informed of new developments by (**9**) _____ memos to all concerned.

---

2 Use the clues below to complete this crossword with words related to communication.

					1		2		3		4
5	6										
						7					
8				9			10				
11							12				
					13			14			
	15		16								
					17						
	18										

Across

2 and 4 down to suggest different products to a customer who is already buying another product (5, 4)

5, 7 down and 9 down direct contact with someone, not over the phone or by Internet (4, 2, 4)

8 and 12 a short form for a recruiting advertisement (3, 2)

9 and 6 down an official letter or statement saying you are sorry (6, 7)

11 a piece of paper put on a wall or on a website giving official information (6)

12 see 8

13 'Let's keep ___ touch.' (2)

15 'Sorry. I haven't called her ____.' (3)

18 If you would like to thank someone formally, you 'express your ____.' (9)

Down

1 the past of 'meet' (3)

3 and 14 When someone is speaking on the telephone they are '___ the ____.' (2, 4)

4 see 2 across

6 see 9 across

7 see 5 across

9 see 5 across

10 a ____ of communication (5)

16 A '____ break' can be taken in the morning or afternoon. (3)

17 abbreviation for computing or information technology (2)

3 A call centre operator is trying to deal sensitively with a customer complaint. Put in the correct auxiliary verb to complete each statement.

do   'll   would   can   may   do   ~~'ll~~   would

0 I 'll see what I can do.

1 I _____ apologise for the delay.

2 If you _____ be kind enough to give me your mobile number, I'll call you back in a few minutes.

3 I _____ understand your worries.

4 _____ 9am be a convenient time?

5 I _____ get back to you as soon as I can.

6 _____ I be of any more assistance?

7 You _____ call me on this number whenever you like.

Pronunciation

4 Native speakers often contract the auxiliaries *have*, *had*, *will* and *would*. Practise saying these phrases.

I'd love to.   I wish I'd known.

I'll call you.   I've met her before.

If I'd had more time, I'd 've visited you.

She'll 've finished by this afternoon.

Verb patterns

5 Match each verb on the left with the one closest in meaning on the right.

0 thank	A invite
1 promise	B convince
2 urge	C be grateful
3 suggest	D blame
4 persuade	E discourage
5 dissuade	F encourage
6 ask	G undertake
7 criticise	H propose

6 Each pair of verbs in exercise 5 is followed by the same grammatical form. Write the form that follows each.

0 thank and be grateful (to someone) for something **or** for doing something

1 _____

2 _____

3 _____

4 _____

5 _____

6 _____

7 _____

7 Change each of the direct quotations from newspaper reports into reported statements.

0 'It's entirely the fault of the banks. They should have been more open about their charges to customers,' one industry commentator said.

An industry commentator blamed the banks for not being open about their charges to customers.

1 Asked by business leaders what he would do to help them, the finance minister said, 'I will first simplify the tax system and then step by step reduce the burden of tax on companies.'

The finance minister promised _____
_____ .

2 The chairman of Chrysler™ told investors, 'We must be patient. The current downturn is part of the economic cycle and there will be better times again.'

The chairman urged _____
_____ .

3 A source close to the management said, 'It's a really good product, but the world isn't ready for it yet. They should relaunch it in a year or so.'

A source close to the management suggested ___
_____ .

4 Hamilton had these words for his team. 'Everyone has worked very hard and unselfishly to achieve this success.'

Hamilton praised _____
_____ .

5 Fredericks defended the appointment of his son, saying, 'There is no favouritism here; Nigel has got the job purely on merit.'

Fredericks denied _____
_____ .

6 The industry watchdog was less complimentary. 'Degas have put unfair pressure on customers to sign up to new contracts – they haven't broken the rules, but they have bent them!'

The industry watchdog criticised _____
_____ .

7 A spokeswoman from the Consumer Association said, 'Consumers should probably try to avoid buying dairy products from France just at the moment, until more is known about the disease.'

The spokeswoman discouraged _____
_____ .

8 The head of the airline said, 'If the competition continue to drop their prices like this, we will be forced to do the same and then there will be a price war which will benefit no-one.'

The head of the airline threatened _____
_____ .

Reading

8 Read this blog post on how businesses can best exploit social media and then match each statement (1–8) with one of the paragraphs (A–E). You will need to use some of the letters more than once.

The social media challenge

A

Social media is a two-way conversation you need to be part of. No business, not even your local independent hair salon, can afford to ignore social media these days as part of their communication with the outside world. To do so is like putting your fingers in your ears, taking the sign off your shopfront and pulling the blinds down. No-one will know about you and, even if they do take notice of you, you won't have any idea what they're saying about you.

B

OK. We've established that a business needs a social media presence. But what does that actually mean? Social media is not just another marketing channel where you put up an advertisement shouting out what you do. It's more involved than that. People in social media spaces don't want to be shouted at or bombarded with sales messages. They want a subtler, more inclusive kind of communication: a conversation that engages them and that they would like to engage others in.

C

One popular route to building a strong social media presence is content sharing. That is to say, you share the best and most interesting content – related to your industry, of course – that you can find. So in the case of that local hair salon, you put up links to articles showing the latest hairstyles that the rich and famous are sporting. Or you put up a blog by a leading

hairdresser who gives advice on how to look after damaged hair. With luck, such posts will provoke and encourage meaningful conversations on your social media pages – ones that genuinely educate visitors.

D

You've got people talking. The trouble is, they're not really talking about you. It's great to have people in the room with you, but let's not forget the whole object of the exercise, which is to bring people to your website or your shopping outlet and from there into the sales pipeline. At the moment, a website focusing on third party content might send users to other people's websites and, who knows, maybe indirectly to a competitor.

E

And there lies the real challenge. To get people listening and talking to you – and ultimately buying from you – you need to create your own style of communication. It will take more than an expert's blogpost or one funny video to get your audience to sit up and pay attention. But if, over time, you can build a bank of coherent, engaging and informative messages with an individual flavour, then people will take notice. And when they do, that is when you will see a return on your investment.

0 Communication channels may have changed, but people are still interested in informative content. *C*

1 The main reason for businesses to use social media is to boost their sales. ____

2 Social media users like to learn something new from the content they read and see. ____

3 The danger of using third party content is that users may buy from someone else. ____

4 Businesses sometimes give social media users the opportunity to connect to other websites. ____

5 A business that doesn't use social media is missing out on an important opportunity. ____

6 Social media allows companies to speak to customers and to listen to them too. ____

7 Social media users dislike receiving advertising communications. ____

8 Getting your social media messaging right is not a simple or quick process. ____

3.2 Email exchange

Formal and informal emails

1 Convert the following formal email into an informal one by changing the underlined words.

● ● ●

Dear Didier

(0) <u>Thank you</u> Thanks for offering to (1) <u>assist</u> me with the Blane report. The chairman specifically (2) <u>proposed that I should</u> compile it and, (3) <u>therefore</u>, I (4) <u>do not</u> feel I (5) <u>am able to</u> accept your kind offer. (6) <u>However</u>, (7) <u>I would be very grateful if you could</u> send me any relevant information that might help me with it. (8) <u>Do not hesitate to</u> call me if you (9) <u>wish</u> to discuss it (10) <u>further</u>.

Kind regards

Jean

---

2 Convert the following informal email into a formal one by changing the underlined words. Use the words in the box to help you (in most cases you will need to use other words too).

> contact   do not   soon   prefer   sincerely
> grateful   will   currently   meantime   apologise
> my apologies   send   ~~thank~~

● ● ●

Dear Ms Doyle

(0) <u>Thanks</u> Thank you for your email. (1) <u>I'm sorry</u> for the delay in sending you the T-shirt that you ordered. (2) <u>At the moment,</u> we (3) <u>don't</u> have the medium size you asked for in stock. We hope to have delivery of these on Friday. (4) <u>The moment</u> they arrive, (5) <u>I'll</u> (6) <u>get</u> one out to you by first class post. Or, if (7) <u>it's better for you</u>, I can send you either a small or large T-shirt of the same design immediately. If this is the case, (8) <u>please</u> (9) <u>get in touch</u> and let me know. (10) <u>For now</u>, I will try to get the medium size in as soon as possible.

(11) <u>Sorry</u> once again.

(12) <u>Best wishes</u>

Gareth Evans

---

3 Choose a linking word or phrase from the box to fill each gap (1–8). (Some words are not needed.)

> since   however   nevertheless   besides
> ~~owing to~~   anyway   in the meantime
> consequently   although   following
> subsequently   moreover

Dear David

In response to your request, I am writing with an update on the construction of the new PB1 headquarters in Shanghai.

(0) *Owing to* difficulties obtaining planning permission, work has not in fact begun yet. As you know, there were some features of the original design which the local planning authorities were not happy with and, (1) _____ , we have had to submit modified plans. We are not anticipating any problems with these changes, but, (2) _____ , we will have to wait for formal permission before starting work.

(3) _____ , we have been able to start construction of the access road to the building. This work is progressing well and will be completed in time for the main construction.

(4) _____ , it will also be on budget.

(5) _____ the withdrawal of Jarjing Inc, one of the building subcontractors, we have had to look for a replacement. (6) _____ , this is not something that we want to rush.

(7) _____ , we already have two subcontractors who can begin the work when permission is granted. (8) _____ we need to find the right partner, we have invited about ten firms to bid for the contract and we expect to make a decision within the next eight weeks.

I hope this gives you enough information. Please do not hesitate to call me if there are further details you require.

Best regards

Mei Ling

3.3 Listening Test: Part One

Predicting what word(s) will go into each space is a key skill in Part One of the Listening Test.

I Study the sentences in the seminar notes below and predict what kind of word(s) will go into each gap. The missing word(s) or phrase(s) might be a date, a name, an adjective, an adverb, a verb phrase etc.

2 Read the statements about Part One of the Listening Test and mark them *True* or *False*.

1 Correct spelling of the missing words is not so important.

2 Don't write the exact words you hear in the recording.

3 It helps to understand the context of the passage first.

4 Don't get stuck on a particular question; you will have a second chance to listen.

5 It's better to leave a space blank than write in a guess.

IMPACTO SEMINAR

Introduction

1 Impacto was founded in _____ .

2 It specialises in improving business people's _____ .

3 Most business people communicate _____ .

4 This is a one-day taster course, but you can follow courses for up to _____ .

Good communication

5 Good communication is about feeling _____ .

6 If you can show this quality, other people will _____ .

7 What we aim to do is bring out your _____ .

8 It's also very important to understand the dynamics of _____ .

The main topics

9 Today we are going to look at dealing with difficult _____ .

10 Everyone finds themselves in situations which are _____ .

11 We will use video case studies, demonstrations and _____ .

12 As you leave you can help yourself to a _____ .

4.1 The art of selling

Selling

1 Match each word on the left with a word on the right to make sales and marketing collocations.

0 prospective	A maker
1 emotional	B advantage
2 buying	C customer
3 unique	D service
4 payment	E technique
5 sales	F terms
6 competitive	G signal
7 price	H benefits
8 decision	I value
9 added	J selling point
10 after-sales	K competition

2 Read the descriptions of each sales promotion medium and then complete its name.

0 Putting a message on company vans or an advertisement on a bus or taxi: vehicle advertising

1 By far the cheapest and most effective form of advertising: w _____ o _____ m _____

2 Typically used for sporting events to raise awareness of the company's brand: s _____

3 Used by companies to sell a particular product at a retail outlet, eg a supermarket: p _____ o _____ s _____ promotion

4 Large advertisements placed by the side of the road to attract the attention of motorists: b _____

5 Cheap form of promotion, but not that effective as most people throw it away: d _____ m _____

6 Increasingly popular form of Internet advertising that relies on people passing the advertisement to friends and colleagues: v _____ m _____

3 Choose the best word (A–D) for each space (1–6) to complete this article about 'Myths in selling'.

1 **'Buyers are liars.'**

I'm constantly amazed how many salespeople use this expression. Do people (**0**) ____ salespeople? Absolutely. But this usually occurs when the sales person has failed to earn that person's trust. Gaining someone's trust means not (**1**) ____ them into making a (**2**) ____ decision. It means focusing your attention on *their* situation rather than trying to (**3**) ____ the sale. Earning trust means treating people with respect and dignity even if they are not prepared to make a decision right now.

2 **'Anyone can be persuaded to buy.'**

I once heard someone say, 'If you have a strong case you will clarify it. If you have a weak case, you will try and (**4**) ____ the other person.' The real key is to determine whether or not the person or company you are speaking to has a genuine (**5**) ____ for your product or service. If they do not, then your best (**6**) ____ is to move on to someone who does need *and* want your particular solution.

0	A lie	B mislead	C falsify	D fraud
1	A attracting	B making	C pushing	D urging
2	A buying	B buyer	C bought	D buy
3	A finish	B end	C close	D do
4	A dissuade	B persuade	C appeal	D win
5	A interest	B request	C need	D want
6	A way	B strategy	C advantage	D terms

Tenses and time phrases

4 Complete this memo from a branch manager of a bank to her marketing director by putting each verb in brackets into the correct tense.

INTERNAL MEMO

TO: David Cooper
FROM: Maria Nieto
SUBJECT: Home insurance offer

Hi David

You (0) *asked* (ask) me for an update on the home insurance offer that the bank (1) _____ (launch) last month. This is what I can tell you based on the data that I (2) _____ (collect) so far.

Since the launch, we (3) _____ (circulate) about 8,000 leaflets to our customers with their monthly statements. Up to now, the response (4) _____ (be) quite low – about two per cent. By response, I mean people who have requested more information. I expect that by the end of the month most of these people (5) _____ (decide) whether to take up the offer or not. I will of course send you these figures.

I have to say, I am not so surprised at the low response. These days, private customers (6) _____ (tend) to go to one provider for all their insurance – car, house, travel, etc – and that means an insurance company.

As you know, currently the bank (7) _____ (look) into the possibility of offering these other types of insurance and I think that when we do, the response will be much better.

I (8) _____ (write) to you again in a couple of weeks to give you a further update. In the meantime, please contact me if you would like to discuss any of the above.

Best wishes

Maria

---

5 Replace the underlined time phrase in each sentence with the phrase from the box that is most similar in meaning.

> currently   in the past   sooner or later
> in the last decade   up to now
> since I was born   ~~these days~~

0 <u>Nowadays</u> people expect their cars to be completely reliable. *These days*

1 <u>So far</u>, we have spent a very small amount of money on advertising. _____

2 <u>Over the past ten years</u>, the price of oil has more than doubled. _____

3 <u>In time</u>, people will realise what a great product this is. _____

4 <u>At the moment</u> we are developing a new range of women's fashion accessories. _____

5 <u>Formerly</u>, I worked as a sales advisor for a large bank. _____

6 I have lived in Berlin <u>all my life</u>. _____

Transitive and intransitive verbs

6 Some of the following sentences use a transitive verb when an intransitive verb is needed and vice versa. Decide which sentences are correct (✓) and which sentences are incorrect (✗).

0 If we fall the number of people working on the project, it won't be finished in time. (*reduce*) **✗**

1 Our chances of finding a solution are decreasing every day. ☐

2 He rose everyone's hopes of getting a bonus and then announced there would be none. ☐

3 The share price dropped quite dramatically when the government cancelled the contract. ☐

4 The quality of TV programmes has reduced a lot since I was a boy. ☐

5 The bank will probably raise interest rates again this month. ☐

6 The size of the engine has been reduced, but it still produces the same amount of power. ☐

7 How can we rise productivity when the staff feel so insecure? ☐

8 When we have a bigger volume of sales, we can think about declining the price. ☐

7 Complete this telephone conversation between a buyer and a supplier of bath towels. The first letter of each missing word has been given for you.

Supplier Hi, Tracey. How's business?

Buyer Very good thanks. The (**0**) trial we ran with your 'Comfort' range went very well.

Supplier So, you'll be (**1**) p _____ an order soon?

Buyer Yes, I'd like to. Just remind me what the (**2**) d _____ time is.

Supplier We're quoting two weeks for items that we have in (**3**) s _____ .

Buyer OK. And my sales (**4**) c _____ is still as agreed, 40%?

Supplier That's right, 40% of the recommended retail price, which is the price you must sell at – you can't (**5**) m _____ up the price further. What kind of (**6**) v _____ of sales are you anticipating?

Buyer I'm expecting to sell a lot. The idea is to get Selman's to carry the range right across their (**7**) c _____ of stores. I'll phone the order through next week.

Supplier That's excellent news. You'll need more (**8**) p _____ material. I'll send you 300 catalogues and six display stands.

Pronunciation

8 Verbs ending *-ed* can be pronounced in one of three ways: /d/ *arrived* /t/ *stopped* /ɪd/ *wanted*.
Look at the following verbs ending *-ed* and say which way each is pronounced.

increased slightly /t/	changed very little
picked up	ended the year
plummeted	reached a peak
recovered slowly	decreased sharply
fluctuated	rocketed
stayed the same	gradually levelled off
developed	recorded a rise
dropped	

9 Match each of the descriptions in the box to one of the graphs below.

> fluctuated wildly ~~recorded a sharp rise~~
> increased steadily   diverged significantly
> developed in a similar way   reached a peak
> remained relatively stable   recovered slightly
> continued on an upward trend with some fluctuations

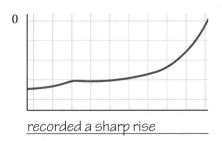

0

recorded a sharp rise

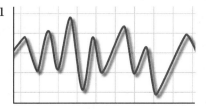

1

_____

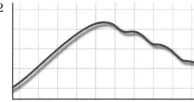

2

_____

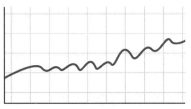

3

_____

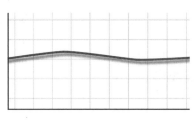

4

_____

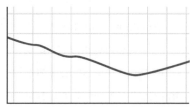

5

_____

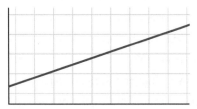

6

_____

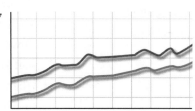

7

_____

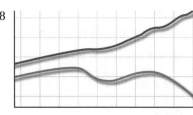

8

_____

4.2 Presenting figures

Describing performance

1 Put the correct preposition in each gap (1–10) to complete the presentation. In some cases more than one answer may be possible.

The graph shows the levels of the country's imports and exports (**0**) *over / during* the period 2006 to 2016. If we look (**1**) _____ imports first, we can see that they increased quite dramatically over the period (**2**) _____ question (**3**) _____ $24 billion to $53 billion. (**4**) _____ contrast, exports fell, though not (**5**) _____ the same extent. From a level of $60 billion in 2006, exports fell to $31 billion in 2016, a fall (**6**) _____ 50%. This was not at all in line (**7**) _____ the forecasts for the economy: the trade surplus of the mid-2000s had been converted (**8**) _____ a trade deficit (**9**) _____ the end of 2015. (**10**) _____ the same time, the country had failed to grow their export market.

2 Complete the sales presentation about two recently launched computer games using the phrases from the box.

As you can see
In conclusion
If we look at the first graph
The second graph shows
Now if there are any questions
Thanks for your attention
Comparing the two
I'm going to present
~~Thank you, everyone, for coming today.~~

(**0**) Thank you, everyone, for coming today. I'm really glad to have this opportunity to tell you how City Cop 2 and Alligator are doing since their launch, and I know that you're all keen to know! So, today (**1**) _____ the results of the first six months' sales. (**2**) _____ , we can see that sales of City Cop 2 were slow at first, but really took off in month three. We don't have any real explanation for this; we're just happy that the market responded. (**3**) _____ , sales have continued to increase rapidly from that time and last month reached 48,000 units. (**4**) _____ sales of Alligator over the same period. This had a good start and recorded a healthy level of sales in the first six months, rising from 16,000 per month to 23,000 units. (**5**) _____ , it's clear that City Cop 2 is on a more rapidly rising curve than Alligator. (**6**) _____ , I would say that the results are very encouraging and pretty much in line with our forecasts. (**7**) _____ . (**8**) _____ , I'll do my best to answer them.

3 Read the questions and answers below. Rewrite each answer in three different ways, beginning as shown. All answers should have the same meaning.

Question: *What effect did the warm winter temperatures have on the ski resort of St Anton?*
Answer: *A lot of people cancelled their holidays.*

0 The result was that a lot of people cancelled their holidays.

1 It resulted _____ .

2 It led _____ .

3 It meant _____ .

Question: *How was such a small company able to compete with the big computer games companies?*
Answer: *They had very talented software designers.*

00 It was because they had very talented software designers.

4 It was on account _____ .

5 It was thanks _____ .

6 It had a lot to do _____ .

4.3 Writing Test: Part One

1 **Decide which of the following tips for answering Part One of the Writing Test are true (T) and which are false (F).**

0 You should begin by describing what the graphs illustrate. T

1 You should use the exact words given in the question to do this. _____

2 You should divide your description into clear paragraphs. _____

3 You should describe in detail the development of each curve. _____

4 You should draw a general conclusion from the information presented. _____

5 You should give reasons for each change in the development. _____

6 You do not need to describe the figures accurately. _____

2 **Answer the following exam question, using the framework given to help you. Then compare your answer with the model answer on page 70.**

Framework

- Begin by describing what the graph is intended to show.
- Describe the general development.
- Describe briefly the development of each of the three curves, comparing them where necessary.
- Write a conclusion about what the graph tells you about the company's activity.

PART ONE

Question 1

- The graph below shows production output at three different plants belonging to the same company over the period 2012 to 2017.
- Using the information in the graph, write a short **report** describing the different rates of production and what this means for the company.
- Write **120–140** words.

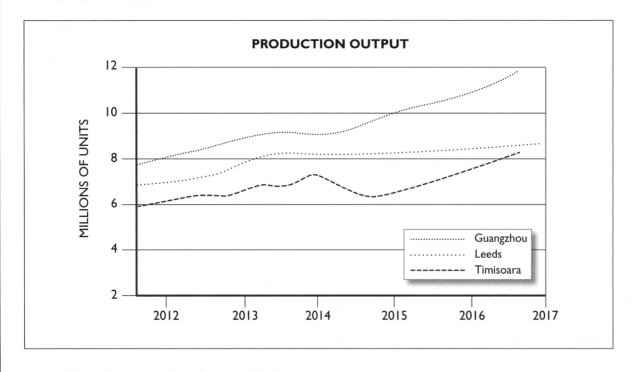

PRODUCTION OUTPUT

MILLIONS OF UNITS

.... Guangzhou
.... Leeds
--------- Timisoara

5.1   Money and finance

Money expressions

1 Choose the best word to complete each sentence.

0 We can't say we have (done) / performed the deal until we have a signed contract.

1 So far, the business hasn't *lent / borrowed* any money from the bank – it's been self-financing.

2 We've *lost / wasted* a lot of money on consultants whose advice hasn't really benefited the business.

3 The company *made / won* most of its profits from the sale of property.

4 I invest on the stock market as a hobby, but I never really *earn / make* any money.

5 I advise you to get a loan from a commercial bank – they *charge / withdraw* less interest.

6 We have *earned / saved* a lot of money by outsourcing our IT services.

7 My house *costs / is worth* twice what I paid for it ten years ago.

8 They *spent / paid* over £1 million developing the new system.

9 I'm not responding to any more orders until they pay us back what they *owe / borrowed* us.

10 How long will it take you to pay *out / off* the loan?

2 Complete the table to show the correct use of the verbs in the box.

| spend   owe   invoice   lend   save   bet   waste |
| ~~pay~~   charge |

pay	someone money **for** something
	money **on** something

3 Complete the dialogue between a bank manager and a customer applying for a loan by writing ONE word in each gap (1–10).

Bank Manager So, (**0**) *how* can I help you?

Customer I'd like to (**1**) —————— out a loan to purchase a business premises.

BM I see. I'll just need to take some details. Is your business a limited company?

C Yes. We've been (**2**) —————— business for five years and we're hoping to expand.

BM How (**3**) —————— are you looking to borrow?

C I've found a suitable property which is (**4**) —————— the market for £350,000.

BM And what is the annual (**5**) —————— of your business?

C Our revenue last year was £294,000. From that we (**6**) —————— an £80,000 profit.

BM That sounds healthy. And what can you offer the bank as (**7**) —————— against the loan?

C I own a house myself which is (**8**) —————— about £400,000.

BM And do you (**9**) —————— any money on that?

C I have about £35,000 left to pay.

BM Well, I don't see any problem. I will need you to fill in this form and also to send me your company (**10**) —————— for the last three years.

Pronunciation

4 Generally we don't stress the articles *a, the, some*; auxiliary verbs *have, can, shall, should*; prepositions *to, from, for, of*. Go through the dialogue in exercise 3 again, on your own or with a partner, and practise saying it without stressing these words.

Bank Manager So, how <u>can</u> (/kən/) I help you?

Customer I'd like <u>to</u> (/tə/) take out <u>a</u> (/ə/) loan <u>to</u> (/tə/) purchase <u>a</u> (/ə/) business premises.

Expressions of comparison

5 The following sentences are all missing one small word. Write it in.

0 This is *the* last time I'm going to tell you.

1 It's a lot bigger _____ I expected.

2 It's _____ more than I wanted to pay.

3 This is _____ far the best example I've seen.

4 I'm not _____ young _____ I used to be.

5 Can you speak a little _____ slowly, please?

6 Can you speak a little _____ quickly, please?

6 Complete the table of comparative and superlative forms.

Adjective (or adverb)	Comparative form	Superlative form
clever	cleverer	the cleverest
good		the best
quickly		
tiring		the most tiring
bad	worse	
well (adverb)		
far		
little		the least
much	more	

7 Look at the table below and then use the prompts to make sentences about the information in the table.

China / by far / population

China has by far the biggest population of all the countries in the table.

1 Life expectancy in Japan / much / in Kenya

2 Japan / slightly / population / Mexico

3 Kenya's inflation rate / very similar / Russia's

4 The number of Internet users in Mexico / much / France

5 Egypt's GDP / not nearly / Russia's

6 China / Mexico / exactly / life expectancy

7 Japan / very / number of Internet users / compared / its total population

8 The USA / by far / country in the table

9 Inflation in Egypt / much / other countries

10 France's unemployment rate / three times / Japan's

Country	GDP per capita $	Population	Unemployment rate	Inflation rate	Life expectancy	Internet users
China	14,600	1.37 billion	4%	2%	76	688 million
USA	57,300	324 million	4.7%	1.3%	80	240 million
Russia	26,100	142 million	5.3%	5.8%	71	105 million
Japan	38,900	126 million	3.2%	-0.1%	85	118 million
Mexico	18,900	123 million	3.6%	2.8%	76	70 million
Egypt	12,100	94.6 million	13%	12.1%	73	32 million
France	42,400	66.8 million	9.7%	0.3%	82	56 million
Kenya	3,400	46.7 million	40%	6.1%	64	21 million

Company finance

8 Complete the brief descriptions of the main three types of financial statement by putting one financial term in each gap (1–10). The first letter has been given for you.

The balance sheet shows the company's
(**0**) assets on one side and its
(**1**) l _____ plus the shareholders'
(**2**) e _____ on the other. The two totals are always equal to each other.

The income statement or (profit and
(**3**) l _____ account) shows the
(**4**) t _____ (and other income) of the company less all its operating
(**5**) c _____ (or expenses). The result is the (**6**) g _____ profit. When tax and interest have been deducted you have the
(**7**) n _____ profit, which is the
(**8**) b _____ line.

The cashflow statement shows the money available to the company at a given time to pay its
(**9**) c _____ and to finance new
(**10**) i _____ .

9 Below is an article giving advice to small business owners. Choose one sentence (A–H) to go in each gap (1–6). (One sentence is not needed).

Eight winning tips to make your financial plan profitable

Create a financial plan: Estimate how much revenue you expect to bring in each month, and project what your expenses will be. If you need it, get help from business planning books, software, (**0**) F.

Review the plan monthly: Even if time is taken to prepare a financial plan with profit and loss projections, it often sits in a desk drawer. (**1**) _____ ; you have to review it regularly.

Lost profits can't be recovered: When comparing your projections to reality and finding earnings too low or expenses too high, the conclusion often is, 'I'll make it up later.' The problem is that you really can't make it up later. (**2**) _____ .

Make adjustments right away: If revenues are lower than expected, increase efforts in sales and marketing or look for ways to increase your rates. If overhead costs are too high, find ways to cut back. There are other businesses like yours around. (**3**) _____

Think before you spend: When considering any new business expense, including marketing and sales activities, evaluate the increased earnings you expect to bring in against its cost before you proceed to make a purchase.

Don't be afraid to hire: Retailers and restaurateurs wouldn't consider operating without employees, but many service businesses limit themselves by being understaffed. (**4**) _____ . You can better use your talents for generating revenue than for running errands and filing.

Pay yourself a salary: If you are incorporated, you may already be doing this. (**5**) _____ . Each month that your business meets its profitability goal, pay yourself the full amount. When you miss your target, dock your 'pay' and when you exceed it, pay yourself a 'bonus'.

It's about profit, not revenue: It doesn't matter how many thousands of dollars you are bringing in each month if your expenses are almost as high, or higher. (**6**) _____ . Don't be one of them.

A Almost any business can benefit from hired or contracted help.

B Every month profits are too low is a month that is gone forever.

C When you get your annual tax bill, it may be too late.

D If not, allocate an amount to owner's compensation on a monthly basis.

E It's not enough to have a plan.

F or ask an accountant

G What is their secret for operating profitably?

H Many high-revenue businesses have gone under for this very reason.

10 Write down six different types of cost a manufacturing company has.

Overhead costs
Marketing costs

5.2 Discussing options

I Write a phrase or sentence to:

0 give your opinion
  As I see it, we should ...

1 ask for someone's opinion

_____

2 make a suggestion

_____

3 state a preference

_____

4 agree with someone

_____

5 disagree politely

_____

6 suggest an alternative course of action

_____

2 Complete each recommendation using one of the endings on the right.

0	My preference would	A	rush into making a decision.
1	I think it would be better	B	about entering the Chinese market.
2	I have some reservations	C	be to develop our markets on all fronts.
3	We shouldn't	D	for the eastern European market.
4	The advantage	E	the best opportunity.
5	We would be better	F	that we wait a year.
6	I think China represents	G	to expand slowly.
7	I suggest	H	off concentrating on Europe.
8	Personally, I would go	I	of Hungary is that it's near.

3 Complete the conversation between a managing director and his deputy director by adding the deputy director's responses from the box in the correct order.

- Maybe, in the short term, but if we were to pass the cost on, we might lose customers.
- That's the decision you have to make, but you've heard my opinion now.
- As I see it, we've got two options. We could absorb the cost or pass it on to our customers.
- ~~What do you want to know exactly?~~
- I'd recommend absorbing the cost for now. The price of steel may come down again.

MD I wanted to ask your advice about the rise in steel prices.
DD *What do you want to know exactly?*
MD Well, what do you suggest that we do about it?
DD _____

_____

MD And which of those two do you recommend?
DD _____

_____

MD My only reservation about that is that it will hurt our profit margins.
DD _____

_____

MD I see what you're saying, but wouldn't it be better to lose a few than to be unprofitable?
DD _____

_____

5.3   Listening Test: Part Two

I   Read the transcript of the Listening Test, Part Two. Complete Task One as you read each extract the first time; then read the extracts a second time and complete Task Two.

- Read the extracts from five business owners talking about their financial situation.
- For each extract there are two tasks. For Task One, choose the sector their business is in, from the list **A–H**. For Task Two, choose the financial problem each person identifies from the list **A–H**.

TASK ONE – SECTOR

1 _____
2 _____
3 _____
4 _____
5 _____

    A car repair
    B clothes retail
    C tourism
    D footwear
    E education
    F property / real estate
    G electrical goods retail
    H mail order firm

TASK TWO – FINANCIAL PROBLEM

1 _____
2 _____
3 _____
4 _____
5 _____

    A high material costs
    B investment risk
    C expensive premises
    D no credit rating
    E high cost of advertising
    F being paid late
    G loans to repay
    H high salaries to pay

Transcript

1   Unfortunately for us, most of our business comes from two big clients. Even though we are only a small group of teachers and trainers, we still have to respect these companies' payment terms. In the case of one of them it's 45 days, and the other is 60 days, which gives us real problems with cashflow.

2   As a high-street shop, cashflow is not a particular problem. It's the rent and local business rates that are so crippling. But because we sell ladies' fashion, location is very important. We could find something much cheaper out of the city centre, but our income would certainly suffer.

3   We borrowed quite a lot of money to set up the business four years ago and I've no regrets. We couldn't have fitted out the garage with the right equipment otherwise – hydraulic ramps, a body-paint shop and so on. It's just that the interest is so high and it means we spend a lot of our time working to service the debt rather than developing the business.

4   It's a great business with very low costs on the whole. We don't have a shop front – we just send out catalogues and people phone in their orders. It can be expensive when we get returns, but the main difficulty is the marketing, because it's so expensive these days. Unless we are present every week in some newspaper or magazine, or on a billboard somewhere, customers forget about us.

5   We are currently buying a lot of small villas and farmhouses in … Well, I won't tell you where in case you get ideas of your own – but it's a small developing country. It's a big gamble, because no-one actually knows whether the market there is going to take off or not. If it doesn't we'll be bankrupted … but I'm confident.

6.1 Purchasing power

Purchasing and supplier relationships

1 Read the extract from an article about consumer protection and choose the best word (A, B, C or D) to fill each gap (1–10).

Ninety-six per cent of all shopping transactions go (**0**) _____ . But what protection do you have as a consumer from an (**1**) _____ seller? If you buy (**2**) _____ goods you have the right to return them to the seller within seven days and get a full (**3**) _____ refund. Within 28 days you can obtain a credit note for your unwanted purchase. In cases of (**4**) _____ in receiving goods or finding that the goods were not as advertised, you will have more trouble. Even if you have paid (**5**) _____ and acted in good faith, there is no guarantee the seller will do the same. An online trader might, for example, sell you something he doesn't have (**6**) _____ stock. When you complain, he might answer that there has been a 'slight delay in (**7**) _____ ' and there is little you can do. In the end, if you cannot get satisfactory compensation from the supplier, then your only option is to take your case to a consumer association or small claims court. Unsurprisingly, most people don't bother. They just tell their friends to (**8**) _____ of the company in future.

But what happens if you feel that you have been (**9**) _____ for a product or service? This is a situation that, up to now, even the small courts have not been able to help with. However, in a recent court case, a large sportswear retailer was found guilty of selling football shirts at an (**10**) _____ price and fined a six-figure sum.

0	A (smoothly)	B on	C fluently	D properly
1	A impartial	B unsure	C unreliable	D inept
2	A fallible	B false	C failing	D faulty
3	A exchange	B cash	C monetary	D money
4	A deliveries	B delays	C postponements	D pauses
5	A promptly	B fast	C accurately	D off
6	A at	B on	C in	D with
7	A distribute	B departure	C dismissal	D despatch
8	A beware	B avoid	C distrust	D suspect
9	A overpriced	B oversold	C overcharged	D overdone
10	A excess	B above	C unreasonable	D increasing

2 Complete each definition by writing one word in the gap. The first letter has been written in for you.

0 When you telephone a supplier to order goods or services you place an order.

1 If you wish to continue a contract or agreement on the same terms you ask for an e _____ .

2 Discounting products at certain times of the year, is known as s _____ discounting.

3 A company which uses its purchasing power to force its suppliers to give better and better prices is said to be s _____ them.

4 Materials in their basic state used in manufacturing are called r _____ materials.

5 A contract to be the only agent representing a supplier is called an e _____ contract.

6 If, when your material costs increase, you increase the price to the final customer, then you p _____ the increase on.

7 The conditions in a contract stating when and how a supplier will be paid are called the payment t _____ .

8 The reaction of customers to a particular product or service is known as customer f _____ .

Reduced relative clauses

3 A *competitive tender* is when a company invites various suppliers to quote for a job. Put these steps in the tendering process into the correct order and number them 1-6. (Use a dictionary if you are unsure of any of the terms in italics.)

The owner / commissioning company
☐ Evaluates the *bids / offers*; makes *a shortlist*
☐ *Awards* the contract to a supplier
☑ [1] Launches *a call for tender*, giving the *technical* specifications

Supplier
☐ *Wins / loses* the contract
☐ *Bids for / tenders for* the contract
☐ *Negotiates* the details

4 Read the conditions of a call for tender set out by a company for its suppliers and replace each participial clause with a relative clause for questions 1–4, and vice versa for question 5–8.

0 Suppliers doing more than 50% of their business with us will have to reduce this dependency.
Suppliers <u>who do</u> more than 50% of their business with us will have to reduce this dependency.

1 Any company wishing to be considered must submit their bid by 20 April.

2 Bids submitted after that date will not be considered.

3 Anyone giving inaccurate information will be disqualified.

4 Prices quoted in this initial bid will be treated as negotiable.

00 Potential suppliers who want to find out more details may call 0208 895 6767
Potential suppliers <u>wanting</u> to find out more details may call 0208 895 6767

5 Anyone who questions the terms should contact our contracts office.

6 Companies who are owned by a larger group or parent company must declare this fact.

7 Suppliers who fail to fulfil all the conditions need not apply.

8 The decision which will be made on 14 May will be final.

Tense practice

5 Complete this email by writing each verb in brackets in the correct tense.

Dear Ms Spackman

I (0) *am writing* (write) to ask you a couple of questions about your recently launched call for tender. Actually, this is the second time that we
(1) _____ (submit) a bid to your company and I hope that this time we
(2) _____ (be) successful.

My questions are as follows:

1) The technical specifications are exactly the same as the last time we (3) _____ (tender) for this contract two years ago. Is this intentional?

2) You ask for three references. How recent must these be? We (4) _____ (do) a job of comparable size six years ago, but since then, we
(5) _____ (not / do) anything on the same scale.

For the time being, we (6) _____
(continue) to work on our offer, but I hope to receive your answers before long.

Yours sincerely

Danny Robinson

A letter of complaint

6 Sentences A–F are extracts from letters of complaint. Read each one and match it to the company it is intended for (1–5).

0 A camera manufacturer who has spent three months repairing a camera.   A

1 An employment agency who supplied an inefficient temporary secretary.   ____

2 A building company who left a job unfinished.   ____

3 An online bookshop which keeps sending out the wrong books.   ____

4 A gas company which has sent an incorrect bill.   ____

5 A consultancy firm that has sent a legal advisor rather than a marketing specialist.   ____

A I am writing concerning the unacceptable delay we have experienced.

B I am writing to complain about what I see as serious negligence on your part.

C I think there has been some misunderstanding.

D It is with much frustration that I find myself writing to you yet again about the incorrect filling of an order.

E Re: Ms Davies
I am writing to express my deep concern about the standard of work of the above.

F I would like to draw to your attention the fact that we have been overcharged for our last three months' consumption.

7 A building company you have hired to renovate your offices has left the job half finished to go and complete another job. The consequence is that your employees are working in unsuitable and unsafe conditions. Write a letter of complaint using the framework below. (200–250 words)

Framework
- the reason for writing
- details of the work that you originally agreed
- details of the work that they have actually completed
- the conditions your employees are working in now
- your next course of action
- closing remarks

Pronunciation

8 Look at these groups of words and say which two contain the same vowel sound.

0 (fill)   (bid)   file
 Both contain /ɪ/, file has the sound /aɪ/ as in try.

1 work   walk   learn

2 lawyer   launch   law

3 special   legal   present

4 agent   failure   chat

5 month   honest   front

6.2 Telephoning

Telephone expressions

1 Match each telephoning expression on the left with a phrase on the right.

0	to hold on	A	to call again with the information needed
1	to hang up	B	to phone back
2	to get through to someone	C	to put someone through
3	to return a call	D	to reach someone
4	to get the wrong number	E	to wait
5	to get back to someone	F	to put down the receiver
6	to connect someone	G	to misdial

2 Complete these telephone exchanges using sentences beginning with *I'll ...* .

0 Can I speak to Fanny, please?

Of course. I'll *just get her for you.*

1 His line is engaged. Would you like to hold?

No, that's OK. I'll _____

2 Can I give you the address?

Sure. One minute, I'll _____

3 Can I speak to someone in technical support?

One moment. I'll _____

4 Is the correct figure 7.8 or 8.7?

Hang on, I'll _____

5 I need the information urgently.

OK. I'll _____

6 Please tell Kevin that I will meet him outside 210 Regent Street at 10.30.

OK. I'll _____

7 Do you have the information to hand?

No, but I'll _____

8 So, 6 o'clock tomorrow at the Red Lion pub in George Street.

Great. I'll _____

3 Rewrite this telephone conversation using idiomatic and natural English.

0 **A** Hello, would it be possible to converse with Mr Fernandez?

Hello, Can I speak to Mr Fernandez, please?

1 **B** Yes. If you would be patient for a little while, I will confirm whether he is available.

_____

A Thank you.

2 **B** I would like to tell him your name, if I may.

_____

A Mrs Sarah Jordan.

3 **B** Thank you, Mrs Jordan ... I will transfer your call to his line now.

_____

4 **C** Hello, this is Mr Fernandez. How may I be of assistance to you?

_____

5 **A** I am telephoning you from Mcmillion Publishers. The purpose of this telephone call is to enquire whether you will be attending the book launch this evening.

_____

6 **C** One moment, please. I will consult my diary. I regret that I have another engagement this evening.

_____

7 **A** Don't be concerned. It will be repeated on 12 May. Is that date convenient?

_____

8 **C** Perhaps. I will have to telephone you again when I have more information.

_____

9 **A** It will be a pleasure to hear from you.

_____

6.3 Writing Test: Part Two

1 Read the exam question: What kind of letter are you going to write?

Register:

A formal

B semi-formal

C informal

Tone:

A apologetic

B sympathetic

C firm and unsympathetic

Content:

A accepting full responsibility

B suggesting a compromise

C denying responsibility

PART TWO
Question 1

- You represent a company that makes and fits swimming pools for private customers. A customer has complained that the heater you supplied for his pool is not powerful enough to heat the water sufficiently and is threatening legal action.

- Write a **letter** to the customer:
  - acknowledging his problem
  - pointing out he was originally offered a choice of heaters (and chose a smaller one)
  - explaining that this is not your financial responsibility
  - suggesting other possibilities to rectify the situation (eg a bigger heater)
  - mentioning what the next step is.

---

2 Write in the missing words (1–8) to complete the framework of the letter.

~WaterWorld~

Dear Mr Opik

I apologise **(0)** for missing your recent call concerning your new pool. I was also sorry and surprised to hear that you have **(1)** _____ problems with it so soon.

(2) _____ you will recall, when we originally discussed _____

_____

_____

_____

_____

_____

_____

_____

As a **(3)** _____ of this, we feel that it is not

_____

_____

_____

In **(4)** _____ to resolve this problem, I suggest that _____

_____

_____

If you like, I would be very **(5)** _____ to come

_____

_____

_____

I look forward to **(6)** _____ **(7)** _____ you

Yours **(8)** _____

Selma Chakrabati

3 Complete the letter, adding the necessary details around this framework. Write 200–250 words.

7.1 Managing people

Managerial qualities

1 Complete each phrase (1–10) with the most appropriate ending (A–K).

'The most important thing for a manager to learn is how to ...'

0	recognise and reward	A	responsibility
1	motivate	B	his / her team
2	delegate	C	work efficiently
3	make	D	with all other departments
4	co-operate	E	good performance
5	lead	F	between what is a priority and what is not
6	set	G	quick decisions
7	organise	H	his / her ideas clearly
8	deal with	I	by example
9	distinguish	J	clear objectives
10	communicate	K	difficult people

2 Read the conversations and write the most suitable idiom in each gap (1–8). You may need to make changes, to verb forms or pronouns, for example.

spread oneself very thin	take it on board
put people on the spot	~~hands on~~
bite off more than you can chew	
open a can of worms	cut corners
get on with	get one's hands dirty

'The job is probably more (**0**) hands on than you had in mind. How do you feel about going out to work in the field with a team of engineers?'

'I'm not afraid to (**1**) _____ and generally I (**2**) _____ engineers very well. I was one myself for 20 years!'

'How are you finding working with Ji Sung? He's quite demanding isn't he?'

'Well, he (**3**) _____ quite often, but actually, I like to be challenged. The problem is that he tries to do too many things himself – he (**4**) _____.'

'Look, the boss wants this done properly; the cost is not the first priority.'

'Don't worry, I will (**5**) _____ . We are not going to (**6**) _____ on this job.'

'Are you sure you can find the time to do this? It's a lot of work and I don't want you to (**7**) _____.'

'Finding the time is not what I'm worried about. I'm more concerned that by investigating all these employees' expenses, we are going to (**8**) _____.'

Pronunciation

3 Decide whether the words in each pair below have the same vowel sounds or different vowel sounds.

			same	different
0	know	no	✓	
1	can	can't		
2	board	bored		
3	first	fast		
4	lead	lied		
5	peace	piece		
6	weight	wait		
7	want	won't		

Expressing purpose

4 Read the reasons that different people give for taking an MBA. Complete each one using the expression of purpose in brackets with the correct verb pattern.

0 I did an MBA (so that / be) better prepared for the world of work.
   I did an MBA *so that I would be* better prepared for the world of work.

1 Actually, I did an MBA (avoid / have) to look for a job immediately.

2 My main motivation was (just /understand) business better.

3 I wanted to do an MBA (in order / meet) people from different backgrounds.

4 I waited until I was 33 to do my MBA (so that / get) the maximum benefit from it.

5 I did the MBA just (in case / be) useful in later life.

6 I was sent on an MBA by my insecure boss (prevent / me / take) over his job!

5 Complete the sentences by thinking of ways to improve different aspects of your English.

0 I am going to *take every opportunity to speak English* so that I can become more fluent.

1 I am going to _____ to expand my vocabulary.

2 I am going to _____ in order to improve my pronunciation.

3 I am going to _____ in case I am asked to speak English at a job interview.

4 I am going to make a list of my most common mistakes to avoid _____ .

5 I am going to read more business magazines in order to _____ .

6 I am going to watch more English TV so that _____ .

Word order when using adverbs

6 Rearrange the words to make sentences.

0 I / tomorrow / can / give / certainly / you / an answer
   I can certainly give you an answer tomorrow.

1 She / keeps / rarely / waiting / anyone

2 He / best / under pressure / performs

3 He / at / never / his desk / is

4 If / want / you / properly / something / done / yourself / it / do

5 I / was / exhausted / completely / the trip / after

6 Please / at this address / me / send / every Monday / an update

7 They / next month / their headquarters / to Shanghai / will move

Reading

7 Read the text and underline the phrases in the text which give you the following information:

1 According to the survey, almost 50% of managers believe that …

2 The results of employee surveys show that …

3 The root cause of employee disengagement is …

4 The practice of calculating who are the best and worst employees is …

5 'Bottom slicing' is based on …

6 The key to engaging employees is …

8 Choose the best option to complete the sentences in exercise 7.

1 A the workforce should be cut regularly.

  B 5% of the workforce is lazy.

  C a fifth of the workforce should be fired.

  D targets are more important than jobs.

2 A employees have no confidence in management.

  B employees don't respect their managers.

  C employee morale is high.

  D most employees want to change jobs regularly.

3 A employees not working to their full capacity.

  B people taking unnecessary sick leave.

  C managers not doing their job properly.

  D the economy wasting huge amounts of money each year.

4 A the answer to employee engagement.

  B a popular way to measure performance.

  C a scientific way to measure performance.

  D not as popular as it was a few years ago.

5 A getting rid of the least effective employees.

  B cutting costs in the organisation.

  C making the employees responsible for targets.

  D paying employees less when they underperform.

6 A rewarding good performance.

  B good communication.

  C good planning and strategy.

  D helping employees reach their goals.

What do we do about disengaged staff?

A survey published some years ago by management consultancy firm, Hudson, produced some shocking findings about managers' attitudes to employees. One in six said they thought the company could shed a fifth of its workforce without doing any significant harm to the company's performance or to employee morale. Almost half considered that a regular trimming of 'dead wood' – getting rid of around 5% of the workforce each year – would actually be a positive measure. Firing people, they seemed to be saying, is an effective management tool.

On the other side, surveys of employees show that only 18% feel confident that their employer will look after them. Around a third say they are looking to leave their current job in the next 12 months, and 51% indicate that they are 'not engaged' in their work. Clearly, something has gone wrong in the employee–manager relationship and the result is low staff morale and high staff turnover.

Gallup™, whose latest poll of employee engagement shows that 16.5% of workers in the USA are 'actively disengaged' (feel no commitment to their work or loyalty to their organisation), estimates that this costs the economy around $450 billion a year in low productivity and lost days through sickness. It's difficult to escape the conclusion that the culprit of all this is poor management. Employers are right in thinking that their workforce is not performing as it should; they are just blind to where the real blame lies.

One possible reason for bad management attitude is a historical reliance on performance measurement tools, and in particular forced ranking. Forced ranking is a system where employees are evaluated yearly, and the best and worst-performing employees are identified. What generally follows is what is known as 'bottom-slicing'. Fortunately, this practice is now in decline, but the thinking behind it – that the best way to improve performance is simply to start with a new employee – has not gone away.

The answer to increased employee engagement is not rocket science. As a first step, managers need to put the measuring tools away and talk more to their employees. Talking to employees can mean criticising them for poor work, but it also means praising them when they have done well. It means keeping them informed of the bigger picture: how the company is doing and what its next direction is. You cannot expect someone to be engaged if they have no idea what they are working towards. The art of management, after all, is to get the best out of people: the engaged and the disengaged alike.

7.2 Report writing

A business report

1 The following list contains elements that are all important in report writing. Mark those you think are the essential points (++) and those you think are important (+).

- Answer all the points you have been asked to address accurately. ☐
- Begin with a clear introduction of the aims of the report. ☐
- End with a definite conclusion and recommendation. ☐
- Use sub-headings and bullet points to make the report clearer. ☐
- Be consistent in your arguments and connect your ideas with linking expressions. ☐
- Use language naturally, appropriately and with a minimum of errors. ☐
- Use sophisticated vocabulary and grammatical structure. ☐
- Organise the report so that it is clear which point is being addressed. ☐

2 This report makes some recommendations for a company planning to buy new computers. It is well organised, concise and relevant. But it contains several mistakes in grammar and spelling, which are underlined. Correct the mistakes.

0 *to present*

To: Said Kamal

Re: New computers

The aim of this report is (**0**) <u>presenting</u> the best (**1**) <u>choose</u> for the company in replacing its computers in the central administration offices. Following some (**2**) <u>initially</u> research, we narrowed the field down to three possibilities:

The first, DX590, is the (**3**) <u>more</u> expensive of the three, (**4**) <u>with</u> a cost of $590 per unit. However, it is the most (**5**) <u>powerfull</u> and adaptable. The second, the

HS Venturer, is a little cheaper to purchase, at $555, but has a smaller hard disk capacity and a slower processor. The third, the Songsing AF100, is (**6**) <u>the</u> bargain at $480 and has similar specifications to the HS Venturer. However, Songsing is a relatively new company and thus it is difficult (**7**) <u>getting</u> references for the product.

(**8**) <u>The another</u> very important factor is the after-sales package. (**9**) <u>Every</u> three companies offer between one- and three-year service (**10**) <u>garantees</u>, but on slightly different terms and at different prices. The best of these is the DX590's two-year warranty, (**11**) <u>that</u> is an on-site 24-hour repair service.

In conclusion, we recommend (**12**) <u>to purchase</u> the DX590. The HS Venturer offers much less for a similar price, while the Songsing AF100 is probably too risky, because it has (**13**) <u>any</u> track record. With good service back-up, the DX590 (**14**) <u>can</u> also prove to be the most economical (**15**) <u>on</u> the long run.

3 Connect the ideas in this report with a linking phrase from the box. (Some phrases are not needed.)

on the whole	due to	although	however
in conclusion	since	indeed	consequently
~~Thirdly~~			

(**0**) *Thirdly*, there is the Giordano Centre in York.
(**1**) _____ we didn't have a lot of time to visit, what we saw impressed us. There are quite a few suitable hotels in the area, all within easy walking distance of the conference centre.
(**2**) _____ , they are reasonably priced.
(**3**) _____ , bookings would have to be made early, (**4**) _____ demand for rooms rises quite dramatically in the summer season. (**5**) _____ , this seems to be the case with all the venues under consideration, so an early decision is recommended.

7.3 Reading Test: Part Two

Do Part Two of the Reading Test. Give yourself 10–12 minutes to complete the task.

PART TWO

- Read this text about work–life balance.
- Choose the best sentence (**A–H**) to fill each of the gaps (**1–6**).
- Do not use any letter more than once.
- There is an example at the beginning, (**0**).

Work–life balance? Easier said than done.

The idea that you can achieve a balance between your work and the rest of your life is predicated on the notion that your work is something distinct from the rest of your life. (**0**) C. For most of us, life is made up of disparate periods of time that we spend at home with the family, at leisure, with friends and at work. Each of us divides our time according to our priorities, spending the bulk of our time on what seems to be the most important thing to focus on at the current time. And for many people, that means work. (**1**) _____

The advocates of work–life balance are very keen to stress its benefits to your health and social life. (**2**) _____ If you spend more time at home or at leisure, then you are by definition going to spend less time working. (**3**) _____ Your employer certainly won't pay you more for putting in fewer hours. And when it comes to promotions, it is reasonable to assume that they are much more likely to favour your colleague who wouldn't dream of missing a meeting to attend his daughter's school play. (**4**) _____

In spite of all the hype about wanting employees to have a good work–life balance, the truth is that job competition has driven us in the opposite direction. If you are not able to stay late three days in a row to get a job finished, there is someone out there who will. The competition could be local. (**5**) _____ A software engineer in India might very well be happy to put in 14-hour days to iron out the glitches in a piece of software that you haven't had time to correct over the weekend.

So where does this all leave us? The challenge for employees is to organise their time more flexibly to focus on different priorities. That might involve taking a long weekend away with friends one week, but then working the following weekend to catch up on missed work or to put in extra hours to make a deadline. (**6**) _____ You could wait for your employer to put their promises about ensuring a good work–life balance into action. But you may be in for a long wait.

A And that will have consequences for your career – monetary or otherwise.

B A few superhuman people may be able to achieve this.

C But it isn't.

D They are less eager to point out the compromises that it involves.

E How many chief executives or successful entrepreneurs do you know of who spend as much time as they would like with their children?

F Increasingly, it is also global.

G It is work that keeps our families fed and a roof over our heads.

H It could mean answering a few work emails early in the morning when on holiday.

8.1 Being responsible

Environmental problems

1 Read the letter to the editor of the *Financial Times* and answer these questions:

1 What prompted the author to write the letter?

2 What does he criticise supermarkets for?

3 What point does he make about the cost of energy?

4 What does he mean when he says 'for all their "green" talk'?

5 How optimistic does he feel about the future?

CAMPAIGN AGAINST IRRESPONSIBLE ENERGY CONSUMPTION

Sir,

D Krajcek (Letters, March 29) draws attention to the way that large corporations disregard the environment by keeping office lights and air-conditioning on in empty rooms, and leaving electrical appliances such as printers, water coolers and computers on overnight. While he is certainly right to campaign against such wastage, there may be no need to single out big businesses in particular.

All of us are guilty of wasting energy in smaller, less noticeable ways. Anyone who has enjoyed a blast of heated or cooled air by simply walking into a store, will know that energy is being wasted as the doors slide open and close numerous times throughout the day. A quick walk through the shopping district reveals lighted LCD panels advertising goods or services all through the night; streams of chilled air gush over the produce on open supermarket shelves, and in many homes, television sets are left in 'standby' mode and mobile devices are left charging though their batteries are full.

Yes, even my children's generation, for all their 'green' talk, do not practise true energy conservation. To make a significant impact on energy conservation, greater efforts must be undertaken by all of us. Raising the cost of energy is one way to go about it; at present the cost of energy is still too low for people to think deeply about conserving it. We must set aside our own greed for present comfort and convenience, in order to save the planet for future generations.

Unfortunately, few today are practising what has been preached for years, and until energy prices triple or climate change forces us out of our homes, I hold out little hope.

F. Rosignol

2 Underline the phrases in the text that mean:

1 to work to decrease or prevent something

2 only point to (one thing)

3 ease or luxury that one is enjoying at the moment

3 What can businesses do to help the environment? Think of two ways for businesses to be more environmentally conscious in each of the following areas.

Waste:

They can put labels on products with instructions on how to recycle them.

_____

Transport:

_____

_____

Energy:

_____

_____

Suppliers:

_____

_____

4 Match the environmental problem from the box with the correct definition 1–5.

| flooding   drought   smog   ~~hurricane~~ |
| extinction   leak |

0 A violent wind that destroys buildings and trees: hurricane

1 A cloud of air pollution that hangs over big cities: _____

2 The disappearance of a species of animal or plant: _____

3 A long period without rain: _____

4 The escape of a dangerous substance into the local environment: _____

5 An excess of water which submerges roads and buildings: _____

Use of prepositions with statistics

5 The table shows the impressive performance of two uranium mining companies on the Australian stock market. Make sentences about the data using the words given. Make sure you use the correct prepositions.

Price Aus$	Jan	Feb	Mar	Apr	May	Jun
Formetal	3.6	4.2	4.2	4.2	4.8	5.4
Uromin	2.4	2.8	3.2	3.0	3.7	3.6

0 stood / January

Uromin shares stood at $ 2.4 in January.

1 increased / $1.2 / the six-month period

_____

2 stayed / the same level / three months

_____

3 average / both / showed a rise / 50%

_____

4 climbed / $5.4 / the end of June

_____

5 reached a peak / $3.7 / May

_____

Gerund and infinitive

6 Complete these statements by putting a verb (gerund or infinitive) into each gap.

0 Are you able to repair the fault or not? If not, I will go to another garage.

1 It's no use _____ Paolo. He won't know the answer.

2 It's not too late _____ your mind. The job is still available.

3 It takes time _____ a new brand.

4 Stop _____ . Everything will be alright.

5 You can't succeed in business without _____ some risks.

6 It's better _____ a small part of something big than a big part of something small.

7 It's worth _____ £100 extra for a business class seat. It's much more comfortable.

8 I always tell a little joke or story before _____ my presentation.

7 What particular construction do these verbs take after them?

to be committed

to get used

to look forward

to object

_____

Modal verbs

8 Below are some notices and signs from a trade exhibition. Explain what each one means using *may, should, shouldn't, must, mustn't, don't have to.*

> **PLEASE USE OTHER DOOR**

0 You shouldn't use this door.

> **MEETING ROOM 6**
> **Knock and enter**

1 _____

> **No Photography in Main Hall**

2 _____

> **AUTHORISED PERSONNEL ONLY**

3 _____

> **Present badges HERE (except staff)**

4 _____

> **REGISTER HERE**

5 _____

> **Events catalogue Please take one**

6 _____

Corporate social responsibility

9 Complete the list of key elements of corporate social responsibility by matching the two halves of each statement.

Corporate social responsibility means ...	
0 getting involved	A in fighting poverty, unemployment and social injustice
1 being accountable	B for your environment
2 considering	C to growing your business by ethical means
3 taking account	D in projects that benefit the community
4 embracing	E to disclose information
5 taking responsibility	F to the outside world for your actions
6 playing a part	G of the impact of your actions
7 being committed	H the challenge of doing business in a sustainable way
8 being prepared	I the welfare of your employees

10 Complete the text by writing ONE word in each gap (1–6).

Our mission at GBD is to build technological solutions (**0**) *that* can transform people's lives for the better. (**1**) _____ a socially responsible company, we are committed to delivering these solutions in a sustainable way.

In this 2017 corporate social responsibility report, you will find all (**2**) _____ information you need relating (**3**) _____ the impact of our activities. It also contains descriptions of the social and environmental initiatives we (**4**) _____ taken in the past year. We are particularly proud of the programmes we have set (**5**) _____ to support science and technology education in local schools. We would like to thank our employees for giving their time and dedication to this work. These programmes typify (**6**) _____ our company is all about and are a key reason why GBD enjoys such loyalty from its employees.

11 Complete the table.

Adjective	Noun
accountable	*accountability*
sustainable	
	injustice
poor	
	environment
committed	
involved	
	respect
	benefit
honest	
	consideration

Pronunciation

12 Check your pronunciation. Mark where the stress falls in each of the words in exercise 11. (You will find the rules in Unit 2 helpful.) Check for other rules on the answer page when you have finished the exercise.

ac**cou**ntable   accounta**bi**lity

8.2 Formal meetings

1 Think of a suitable phrase for each of the following situations in a meeting:

0 Everyone is present and you want to start.
OK. Shall we start?

1 You want to know what points are going to be discussed.

2 You want to interrupt the person speaking to make a comment.

3 You want to stop (politely) another person interrupting you.

4 You want to get on to the next point in the meeting.

5 You think it's time for a break.

6 You think that the discussion has got stuck on one point.

7 You want to praise someone for their contribution.

8 You want everyone to hurry up before the meeting ends.

9 You want another person to answer a question that has been directed at you.

10 You want to conclude the meeting.

2 The following extract is taken from a discussion at a meeting on business ethics. Put the missing phrases into each gap (1–6).

> If I understand you correctly
> That's a good point   could I just finish
> ~~I'd like to come in here~~
> I think Kate is better placed to answer that
> If I could just interrupt
> we should move on to the next item on the agenda

Dean John, I think you had a point to make about misselling.

John (**0**) Yes, I'd like to come in here. We have never had any written code of conduct for sales people; we have just assumed that …

Sarah (**1**) ——————— , that's not true, actually. We do have the handbook …

John Sorry, Sarah, (**2**) ——————— ? We have a selling handbook, but we don't have any code of ethical conduct for salespeople and I think that a lot of them don't really know what the boundaries are in persuading customers to sign a contract with us.

Dean (**3**) ——————— , John. OK, I think we're all agreed on that now. Time is a little short and (**4**) ——————— . That's the question of breach of confidence. Some customers have complained that we pass on information about them to other companies. Sarah, do you have a view on this?

Sarah Actually, (**5**) ——————— . She's responsible for the customer database and marketing.

Kate Well, customers are always asked on the phone if they object to our giving their names to other companies for marketing purposes. If they are registering online then they have to tick a box to opt out of third-party marketing. Perhaps that is where the problem lies.

Dean (**6**) ——————— , you're saying that an opt out may be unethical … that we should give them the chance to opt in, instead.

Kate No, that's not really what I meant. I think …

8.3 Reading Test: Part Four

Do Part Four of the Reading Test. Give yourself ten minutes to complete the task.

PART FOUR
Questions 1–10

- Read this article about ethical investing.
- Choose the correct word (**A, B, C** or **D**) to fill each gap (**1–10**).
- There is an example at the beginning (**0**).

Ethical investing is when an individual or company uses ethical considerations as the main (**0**) _____ for selecting which stocks and securities they will invest in. Usually, this involves eliminating companies that (**1**) _____ in certain activities deemed to be damaging to either people or the environment. These include activities such as gambling and weapons sales or energy production using fossil fuels.

Direct investors make these choices (**2**) _____ themselves, but most investments are made via brokers or fund management companies. They use ethical indices to determine which funds (**3**) _____ as being ethical.

An ethical index will include various key areas in corporate practice:

- Treatment of employees:
  Are they (**4**) _____ remunerated? Are working hours and conditions reasonable?

- Customer relationships:
  Are products priced competitively? Are customer complaints (**5**) _____ in a fair and timely manner?

- Supplier relationships:
  Are all dealings honest (ie no illegal payments are being made)? Does the company (**6**) _____ putting its suppliers under undue pressure?

- Respect for the environment:
  Does the company try to minimise pollution and waste? Does it respect environmental laws and regulations?

- Communication with the outside world:
  Is the company (**7**) _____ about its activities and their impact?

The use of indices ensures that ethical investors focus not only on the negative actions of companies, but also the positive ones. So, (**8**) _____ of discounting an entire industry, like the chemicals industry, investors can encourage companies within such industries which are doing their (**9**) _____ to improve their business practices.

It is also important to remember that ethical investing principles do not only apply to direct investing. We should all be aware, when borrowing money from a bank or paying into a pension scheme, that these funds will be managed by third (**10**) _____ who must select which securities to invest in.

0	A judgement	B criterion	C decision	D rule
1	A concern	B busy	C engage	D work
2	A for	B in	C with	D to
3	A qualify	B succeed	C turn out	D attain
4	A rightly	B accurately	C kindly	D properly
5	A coped with	B got round	C set out	D dealt with
6	A prevent	B avoid	C evade	D avert
7	A obvious	B apparent	C transparent	D visible
8	A rather	B instead	C alternatively	D in spite
9	A most	B best	C hardest	D maximum
10	A organisations	B players	C entities	D parties

9.1   Innovation

Describing products

1 Match each advertising slogan to the correct company.

> fast and efficient service
> innovative state-of the-art designs
> unbeatable value for money
> neat and compact solutions
> up-market designer labels at low prices
> ~~modern functional furniture~~
> reliable quality equipment

21st Century Homes

0   modern functional furniture

SPACE SAVING KITCHENS

1   _____

· R I O C H   A R C H I T E C T S ·

2   _____

PRESTO PRINTING

3   _____

TQ
CLOTHING COMPANY

4   _____

BETTAPRICE FOODS

5   _____

DURAWORK POWER TOOLS

6   _____

2 What is the opposite of each of these adjectives?

0 practical	impractical
1 compact	b _____
2 modern	o _____
3 up-market	d _____
4 value for money	o _____
5 reliable	u _____
6 efficient	i _____

Pronunciation

3 In English the letter 'i' can be pronounced /aɪ/ as in *try* or /ɪ/ as in *trip*. Put the words below into the right column in the table.

equipment	quick	time	image
private	finance	reliable	realise
finish	negative	client	limited
silent	efficient	simple	quality

/aɪ/	/ɪ/
time	quick

Collocations: verb + preposition

4 **Complete the description of a product by putting the correct preposition in each gap (1–8).**

The FX500 PVR is now (**0**) *on* sale (**1**) _____ most electrical stores or online. It consists (**2**) _____ two elements: a digital recorder and DVD player. It comes (**3**) _____ two colours, silver and black, and has a storage capacity of 320GB. Retailing (**4**) _____ just $200, it will appeal (**5**) _____ a first-time buyer rather than the specialist. One excellent feature is the standby saver, which runs (**6**) _____ rechargeable batteries and means that you don't waste electricity when the machine is on standby. Manufactured in Korea, it complies (**7**) _____ US and European standards and is compatible (**8**) _____ almost all makes of TV.

5 **Put the expressions into the right column in the table, according to which preposition comes before them.**

> the world   the same time   the market   home
> a small scale   the pipeline   the end of the day
> the end   the future   holiday   the face of it
> least   practice   average   ~~the moment~~

at	in	on
the moment		

Using *would* effectively

6 **Complete each sentence using *would*, an appropriate verb and the words given in brackets.**

0 If you could make it to the reception, *that would be great* (great).

1 In principle, _____
_____ (no problem).

2 If you could deliver direct, _____
_____ (easier for us).

3 _____
(your invitation), but I'm afraid I have another appointment.

4 _____
(your help), because I don't think I can do it on my own.

5 If I were in your shoes, _____
_____ (the same).

6 Before agreeing anything, _____
_____
(certain guarantees from you).

7 **Make these statements from a negotiation sound more diplomatic by rephrasing them using *would*.**

0 We need your help.
We would appreciate your help.

1 Are you happy to give us a discount?
_____

2 I will have to ask my boss about that.
_____

3 That suits us OK too.
_____

4 That's very difficult for us.
_____

5 We can accept those terms.
_____

6 In exchange, can you guarantee that …
_____

Reading

8 Look at the article by a director of the World Innovation Council and complete the phrasal verbs (1–6) by adding one of the pairs of prepositions.

up with	forward to	up to	up with
out for	out of	~~on with~~	

The importance of innovation

I have spent the last ten years trying to persuade European companies to **(0)** get *on with* the job of innovating and I am **(1)** running _____ patience. Whenever I meet entrepreneurs and inventors, I ask them: 'What is the main obstacle to innovation that you face?' The answer I get in Europe is often the same: companies have cut back on investment because they don't feel the urgency to **(2)** come _____ new ideas all the time. Why not? Because they are already in a dominant position. Of course, they **(3)** look _____ opportunities that might give them an advantage and they do take account of what is needed to **(4)** keep _____ developments in their sector, but in comparison with countries like India and China they don't invest heavily. These countries are **(5)** looking _____ a continuing economic boom. Innovation and scientific research is a key part of this. They know that to **(6)** stand _____ competition from other parts of the world, in the long run it will not be enough just to produce goods cheaply.

9 The two words in each pair below are similar in meaning. Answer the questions to explain the difference between them.

0 Which one uses a product or service and which one buys it?
a customer *buys a product*
a consumer *uses a product*

1 Which one is general and which is specific?
competition _____
competitor _____

2 Which one means *to make something different* and which means *to make a contribution*?
to differentiate _____
to make a difference _____

3 Which one emphasises saving time and money and which one emphasises results?
effectiveness _____
efficiency _____

4 Which means *to reach the same level* and which means *to stay at the same level*?
catch up with _____
keep up with _____

5 Which means *to keep hold of* and which means *to keep up*?
to sustain _____
to retain _____

6 Both give you rights, but which one is like a copyright?
a patent _____
a licence _____

10 Complete each sentence by writing the verb in brackets as a noun or adjective.

0 The challenge is to develop an atmosphere that brings out employees' *creativity*. (create)
1 It's a very _____ product. (innovate)
2 There are leaders and _____ in the industry. (follow)
3 Business _____ is only possible with innovation. (grow)
4 Big _____ on research and development does not always produce big results. (spend)
5 Some good innovations have also been commercial _____ . (fail)
6 Competition is the _____ of innovation. (drive)
7 The idea is not only to win new customers but to retain _____ ones. (exist)

9.2 Negotiating

1 **Read the article and decide whether the following statements are true (T) or false (F) according to the author. If the information is not given in the article write D – doesn't say.**

1 According to Cohen, losing in a negotiation is a bit like losing when playing a game. _____

2 Cohen said that you must enter each negotiation with the desire to win. _____

3 You will only get a good deal if your counterpart knows what is at stake for you. _____

4 People like to negotiate with someone who is calm and confident. _____

5 By caring too much, you open yourself to the possibility of being pushed into a bad decision.

_____

●●●

The famous negotiator Herb Cohen said that in order to negotiate effectively, you have to treat the negotiation like a game. Everyone likes to win at a game, but ultimately, if you lose, it's not the end of the world. To put it another way, he said, you have to 'care, really care .... but not that much.'

Cohen's meaning was that if you want something too much and are not prepared to lose out on it, you will be handicapped. Your counterpart will see how much importance you have attached to getting the thing in question and will extract the highest price possible from you for it.

Caring too much also has a psychological effect. It causes people to become emotional and unpredictable; in other words, it will make you lose your cool. And when you lose your cool, you also lose both the respect of your counterpart and any natural shield that you may have had against emotional manipulation by the other party, regardless of whether said manipulation takes the form of aggressive bullying or sweet-talking you into making the wrong decision.

2 **Complete the dialogue using phrases A–I.**

> A would that be acceptable
> B would you be willing to   C in principle
> D our position is this
> E that's out of the question
> F what did you have in mind
> G Could we meet you half-way   H in return
> I ~~Thanks for agreeing to meet me.~~

A (0)

B It's a pleasure. So, tell me what you are looking for.

A (1) _____ . We have a great product, but no expertise in bringing products to market.

B And if I agree to help you with the marketing ...?

A (2) _____ , we can offer a percentage of profits.

B I see. I would also need a fee for my time; not necessarily the full rate, but something.

A OK, but (3) _____ defer payment for six months?

B No, I couldn't really do that.

A (4) _____ ? A quarter up front, a quarter after three months and the balance after six months.

B I'd have to think about that.

A But, (5) _____ , you would consider it?

B Yes, I'm sure we can find some middle ground. As to the percentage, what are you offering?

A Five per cent. (6) _____ ?

B That's a lot less than I imagined.

A Oh. (7) _____ ?

B More like 25%.

A I'm sorry. (8) _____ .

3 **Match each expression with its definition.**

0 spiral out of control	A begin all over again
1 a stumbling block	B escalate too quickly
2 go pear-shaped	C initial difficulties
3 teething problems	D compromise
4 see it through	E without any problems
5 find some middle ground	F an obstacle to agreement
6 plain sailing	G follow something to its conclusion
7 start from scratch	H go badly wrong

9.3 Reading and Listening Tests: Part Three

The approach to Part Three of the Reading Test and the Listening Test is similar: look or listen for key words to direct you to the relevant part of the passage and then choose an answer which is a paraphrase of what is said in the text.

PART THREE

- Read the article about 'innovation in the car industry' and answer the questions.
- For each question (**1–6**), choose the best answer (**A**, **B**, **C** or **D**).

The Internet of vehicles

Planning for the future is never easy, but when it comes to such a seismic change as the move from a conventional car with an internal combustion engine to an electric or chip-driven car, the task is even more daunting.

There are 1.3 billion cars on the world's roads today, and this is projected to rise to 2 billion by the year 2040. Out of the 1.3 billion, only 2 million are currently electric vehicles, while the rest are still being fuelled by petrol or diesel. The latter rely heavily on an enormous global network of filling stations and fuel supply infrastructure. The opportunity that a shift to EVs (electric vehicles) presents is a chance to completely redesign our cities and for transport networks to be cleaner, quieter and less congested. Cities were never designed in the first place for the huge volume of traffic that they now have to accommodate. Over the years, streets have had to be widened, traffic control and calming measures introduced, and parking spaces found.

It is easy to see how EVs will solve pollution problems. Even though there will have to be investments in new power generation capacity to supply the electricity needed to run the vehicles, these are likely to be greener power plants than those constructed in the past. It is not so easy, however, to see how EVs will reduce congestion and traffic flow; until, that is, you bring self-driving technology – or the 'Internet of vehicles' as it is sometimes called – into the equation.

In the next 40 years, say proponents, the self-driving car will change society more than any other technology in the past century. The theory is that by using cameras, radar and GPS navigation systems, traffic will flow freely without the need for controls. The second idea is that rather than simply replacing traditional cars with electric models, we will use intelligent systems to reduce overall car ownership. By connecting EVs to our own mobile devices, we will be able to arrange car trips in a way that is more convenient for all of us, allowing us to get to our destinations quickly and without any of the hassle that comes with car ownership.

Exactly who will lead this revolution is not entirely clear, but in China – which in 2020 will account for 35% of all new global car sales – there is a lot of talk about the rising 'Internet of vehicles'. Because of China's central planning system, which avoids having different companies compete to own the winning technology, the country is seen as a natural place for this new integrated approach to work.

1 The author implies that the change about to take place in the car industry will be
 A a welcome one.
 B a major one.
 C a necessary one.
 D a painful one.

2 The writer thinks that a move away from petrol to electric vehicles could make our cities
 A more like they were in the past.
 B easier to park in.
 C more carefully designed.
 D more pleasant places to live.

3 According to the author, electric vehicles will help to cut pollution because
 A they don't emit fumes like traditional cars.
 B the cost of electricity will limit their use.
 C they will use environmentally friendly electricity.
 D there will be a limited amount of power to run them.

4 Self-driving cars will mean
 A fewer cars and less external traffic management.
 B more cars but a better flow of traffic.
 C fewer cars and smarter drivers.
 D the same number of cars but fewer journeys.

5 The writer suggests that car sharing
 A has traditionally been arranged using the Internet.
 B is alright if you are not in a hurry.
 C is currently a stressful thing to arrange.
 D usually involves some trouble and effort to arrange.

6 China is well placed to lead the change to a world of new self-driving EV cars because
 A it is the biggest consumer of cars.
 B it has been an important voice in the debate.
 C it uses a single authority to make decisions.
 D it is keen to have a competitive car industry.

10.1   Travel and entertainment

Business travel

1 Read the interviews with two executives about business travel. Match the actions to the right person: Amy Chiu or Harvey Dawes or both.

0 books travel trips by themselves   Amy

1 has their own car   _____

2 travels business class   _____

3 uses public transport   _____

4 is cost-conscious when travelling   _____

5 tries to use non-polluting forms of transport   _____

6 likes sampling local culture, especially the food   _____

7 doesn't like staying in big hotels   _____

8 likes business relationships to be professional   _____

Amy Chiu is a portfolio manager at a wealth management company based in Hong Kong. She travels all around the world to meet clients.

'I have my own travel budget – luckily, it's quite generous – and I book practically all my travel myself. The days of admin assistance in that area have long passed. A lot of my trips are long-haul to places like New York, Zurich and so on. I try to fly overnight whenever I can so that I can sleep on the plane and feel fresh when I arrive. Fortunately, I'm a good sleeper and the business class reclining seats are very comfortable these days. It's very important for me to be at my best when I meet clients, because there's often a lot riding on these meetings.

'I used to own a car, but now that I live in Hong Kong, I don't anymore. It's not about the environment; it's just the practicality of it. You'd be crazy not to use public transport here. The subway train system is just fantastic. I can be at work within 20 minutes of leaving my apartment. And anywhere else I travel to tends to need a plane anyway.

'I like small, boutique hotels. Because I'm away from home so much, I try to find places that feel more like home than big commercial hotels. The problem with the big hotels is that they're all so soulless and identical: you feel you could be anywhere, rather than in a specific part of the world. My favourite is the Einstein Hotel in St Gallen in Switzerland. It's right near the old medieval centre of the town and is very comfortable. I find it a very easy place to do business too: professional, well-organised, straightforward. The Swiss don't really mix business and pleasure.'

Harvey Dawes is the managing director of a renewable energy start-up. He travels around the UK and also visits Germany and China regularly to meet suppliers of photovoltaic panels.

'I do own a car – a Toyota Prius hybrid – but I try to use public transport as much as I can. My car is very economical and not especially polluting when compared to other vehicles, but I guess it's a matter of principle. I don't believe that people should drive if they can avoid it, especially if it's only going to be them in the car. My pet hate is single drivers driving those big 4X4s.

'When I'm travelling abroad, I generally book the cheapest flight I can find, although I am a little particular about which airlines I fly with. I've never been a great flyer and I want to know that I'm in good hands, so I always look at customer reviews of airlines first. As for sitting in business class, I don't really see the point; you don't get there any quicker, do you? Anyway, I couldn't justify the cost, even on some of the longer trips I do. I can't just say 'the company's paying' because well, it's my company after all.

'It's the same with hotels – I don't need anything upmarket, but the location is important. I really dislike big corporate hotels, especially airport hotels and ones on the edge of town where you're miles from anywhere. I generally look for something that's good value for money somewhere central. That way I can explore a bit in the evening or go out to a nice local restaurant. I love trying out new dishes and I certainly get the opportunity to do so when I'm in China. The food is so different from anything you can find here.'

Future forms

2 Three people are sitting in a restaurant. None of them has been served yet. A fourth person arrives and asks them: 'What are you going to eat?' Each one describes his / her choice, but using a different future form. Explain why. (Think about: the timing of the decision, the menu, the waiter.)

   A Ummmm ... I think I'll have the steak.

   B I'm going to have the lobster.

   C I'm just having some soup.

3 The CEO of a manufacturing company is discussing his schedule with his private secretary. Complete the dialogue by writing the verb in brackets in the correct future form.

   S So, just to run through your diary for next Monday. You (**0**) *are having* (have) a working breakfast with the board from 8 to 9.30am. Then there (**1**) _____ (be) a conference call with the heads of the four subsidiaries scheduled for 10am. You (**2**) _____ (meet) the Minister for Industry for lunch at the Carlton at 1pm. What (**3**) _____ (you / say) to him, by the way?

   CEO I (**4**) _____ (tell) him that unless the government (**5**) _____ (give) financial support for a new factory in the north-east, we (**6**) _____ (have) to look for sites outside the UK.

   S He (**7**) _____ (not / like) that.

   CEO Maybe not, but that's the reality. What (**8**) _____ (happen) in the afternoon?

   S You (**9**) _____ (host) a question and answer session at the London Business School at 3pm.

   CEO Who (**10**) _____ (be) there?

   S The audience is mostly MBA students and on the panel there (**11**) _____ (be) two other CEOs, Dave Gardner and Joanna Browne.

   CEO Oh, good, I like Joanna. When (**12**) _____ (it / end)? I was hoping to get some work done at some point!

   S By 4.30pm. Your car (**13**) _____ (bring) you back here afterwards.

   CEO And you haven't made any arrangements for the evening?

   S No.

   CEO Good, I (**14**) _____ (try) not to get home too late.

Events management

4 In the following dialogues people are discussing arrangements for events. Choose the best words to complete each dialogue.

1

A When our one millionth customer walks through the door, we'd like to (**0**) remember / (commemorate) / memorise the occasion with a special presentation.

B That's a good idea, but we need to get good (**1**) advertising / publicity / advertisement from it. I don't think the shop itself is a great (**2**) site / premises / venue for a presentation ceremony. It could (**3**) reflect / look / return badly on us.

A Nonsense. We can (**4**) put up / put on / put off a good show here without having to change too much around.

B And what's the prize going to be?

A I thought we could have a little (**5**) reward / gratitude / presentation ceremony, with the winner getting a year's free groceries.

2

A I am very conscious of the fact that since the merger we haven't had any real social event for the two teams to (**1**) go / become / get to know each other better.

B No, you're right. It would be good to break the (**2**) ice / barriers / frost a bit.

A Yes, and also to give them a bit of a (**3**) favour / treat / pleasure. Everyone has been working incredibly hard over the last four months.

B What did you have in mind?

A Drinks and a meal, perhaps a bit of cabaret. Could you get a rough (**4**) valuation / estimate / calculate of what that would cost and get back to me?

B Sure. How many do you think would (**5**) turn out / turn in / turn up? 50? 60?

go and get

5 Decide whether these phrases are used with *go* or *get* and write them in the correct column.

~~ready~~   to know someone   ~~wrong~~   married
missing   lost   crazy   tired   bankrupt
people involved   to plan   over budget   started
quiet   shopping

go	get
wrong	ready

6 Choose eight of the phrases from exercise 5 and make sentences with them.

I need to get ready for the meeting. It starts in five minutes.

Pronunciation

7 Read the information in the box then put the invisible linking consonants into these phrases.

> **Linking consonants**
> - Often, in English, words that begin with a vowel are linked to the consonant at the end of the word before.
>
>   *get over it* → ge‿tove‿rit
> - If the preceding word ends with a vowel, an 'invisible' consonant is put in.
>
>   *go into it* → go‿w‿into‿w‿it
>   *I am open to ideas* → I‿y‿a‿mopen to‿w‿ideas

0 She expects to arrive at 4pm.

  She‿y‿expects to‿w‿arrive at 4pm.

1 The opening will be at 8am.

2 We didn't go out to a restaurant.

3 I am interested, if you are.

4 Can we just go over the agenda?

5 Do you ever lie about your age?

10.2 The language of proposals

The following answer to an exam question is well-organised, has few mistakes and addresses each point in the question. However, it was considered unsatisfactory as a piece of business communication because:
- it was too vague (no specific details or examples);
- it didn't make concrete recommendations.

1 Read the exam question and the answer. Underline the parts of the answer that seem too vague and non-specific.

2 Now improve the answer by adding more specific points in the places you have indicated.

Question 1
- You feel your company's main product or service would benefit from better publicity. The directors have asked you to write a proposal putting forward your ideas.
- Write your **proposal** for the directors:
  - mentioning the product or service concerned
  - stating the shortcomings of the current advertising
  - outlining how your competitors promote their products or services
  - suggesting a different approach to advertising.

To: The directors

I would like to draw your attention to the performance of one of our main products, the energy drink Zap.

Unfortunately, it has experienced some problems in the market, while our competitors' products have improved their sales by an average of 8%. We need to take steps urgently to deal with this situation.

The main problem is our advertising campaign, not the product. We need to find a different way to advertise the product or our product will continue to lose market share to its competitors.

By contrast, they have used innovative styles of marketing and advertising, both on TV and online. In this way, they have attracted a lot of attention and gained new customers. We must do the same, because customers are bored of our advertising.

My recommendations are as follows:
  – we should employ the services of specialists in the field of advertising to help us define a new campaign.
  – we should design some advertisements which feel fresh and attractive and run these on different types of advertising media: TV, radio, social media, billboards etc.
  – we should use some famous people in the advertisements, because this will help to persuade consumers that it is a good product.

Please consider these proposals carefully and do not hesitate to contact me for further details.

10.3 Speaking Test: Part Three

1 Read the prompt card that was given to the candidates in Part Three of the Speaking Test. Make a list of ideas for reducing spending and convincing staff to adopt these ideas.

Business travel

Your company is based in the USA, but has subsidiaries in Europe and China. It sells its products all around the world. Travel is an important part of its activity. However, spending on business travel is too high and you would like to reduce it.

Discuss, and decide together:

- how you could reduce spending on travel
- how you can persuade the staff that such savings are necessary.

---

travelling economy class

_____
_____
_____
_____
_____

point out that reducing travel is environmentally friendly

_____
_____

Useful language

Personally, I think …
In my opinion, …
On the whole, …
I'm not sure: on the one hand, … on the other hand …
You're right.
I agree with you.
Maybe so, but …
No, I don't see it that way. For me, ….

---

2 Look at the transcript of the discussion between two candidates. Improve or correct the underlined phrases.

A So, (**0**) <u>we must discuss the topic</u> of spending on travel. (**1**) <u>What opinion do you have about</u> this question?

  0 *we need to look urgently at the problem*

  1 _____

B (**2**) <u>In my thinking</u>, (**3**) <u>most important</u> is to stop people flying business class. Maybe for the senior directors it is sometimes necessary, because they need to arrive for a meeting feeling fresh after a long flight. (**4**) <u>On another hand</u>, for more junior staff or for short journeys, it is just a waste of money.

  2 _____

  3 _____

  4 _____

A (**5**) <u>I am agree with you.</u> (**6**) <u>It is another true</u> that if we used only one airline for all the flights, we could get a better deal from them. They would give us a better price and (**7**) <u>more</u> perhaps allow us to participate in some kind of loyalty scheme.

  5 _____

  6 _____

  7 _____

B (**8**) <u>I like.</u> We could do the same thing with car hire. If we launch a call for tender for all the car hire worldwide and then choose the lowest bidder, we are sure to make savings.

  8 _____

A So, (**9**) <u>if I can do a summary of these points</u>, we (**10**) <u>agreed</u> that we should look first at air travel …

  9 _____

  10 _____

3 Think of three or four follow-on questions that the examiner might ask.

Do you think that with modern telecommunications, business people don't really need to travel at all?

11.1 The economy

Economic issues

1 Read the text about two different visions for the US economy and answer the questions.
What did the candidates say about …

- taxation?
- economic groups needing help?
- work and jobs?
- trade?

In the 2016 US presidential campaign, the two candidates presented very different visions for the economy. Hillary Clinton proposed taxing the rich and corporations more and giving work incentives to the middle class. 'If you work hard and do your part,' she said, 'you should be able to get ahead.'

Donald Trump, on the other hand, suggested that the problem with the economy was high taxes, over-regulation and globalised business. He proposed helping the working class by bringing manufacturing jobs back to America.

'Our politicians have aggressively pursued a policy of globalisation – moving our jobs, our wealth and our factories overseas. If we lower our taxes, remove destructive regulations, unleash the vast treasure of American energy, and negotiate trade deals that put America first, then there is no limit to the number of jobs we can create.'

2 Cross out the word that doesn't collocate with the word in bold.

0 **economy**: depressed / ~~heavy~~ / stagnant

00 **unemployment**: rate / benefit / ~~credit~~

1 **living**: cost of / standard of / quality of

2 **economy**: blooming / booming / buoyant

3 **sector**: private / civil / public

4 **market**: job / labour / work

5 **trade**: excess / deficit / surplus

6 **tax**: burden / bill / load

7 **consumer**: faith / confidence / spending

8 **government**: present / subsidy / grant

9 **power**: consuming / buying / purchasing

3 Match the words A–G, ending *-less*, to the correct definitions 1–6.

0	having no idea	A	homeless
1	nowhere to live	B	speechless
2	of no value	C	clueless
3	unemployed	D	worthless
4	unable to reply	E	penniless
5	showing no pity	F	ruthless
6	in complete poverty	G	jobless

4 Match the prefixes on the left with A–I to make words.

0	under	A	fidence
1	re	B	courage
2	en	C	petition
3	de	D	locate
4	dis	E	employment
5	com	F	mine
6	con	G	efficiency
7	in	H	pressed
8	un	I	abled

Conditionals (types 1 and 2)

Remember!

Type 1 *If* + present, ... *will* + infinitive = real and possible

Type 2 *If* + past, ... *would* + infinitive = unreal or improbable

5 **Use type 1 or 2 conditionals to complete the sentences, using the verbs in brackets.**

0 If I *were* (be) you, I *would be* (be) very careful.

1 If you _____ (not / mind), I _____ (leave) a little early to catch my train.

2 If the exchange rate _____ (be) better, we _____ (do) a lot more business with them.

3 I _____ (not / have) any supper, if it _____ (be) OK with you. I had a big lunch.

4 She _____ (find) people more helpful, if she _____ (be / not) so rude.

5 If the government really _____ (want) people to use their cars less, it _____ (triple) the price of petrol.

6 I _____ (take) the job if I _____ (think) I had the right skills.

7 Do you think that he _____ (mind) if I _____ (borrow) his car?

6 **Use an *if*-clause to explain why you would do the following:**

0 miss a day's work   *if I felt really unwell*

1 go into work when you were sick

_____

2 accept a gift from a client

_____

3 refuse a job promotion

_____

4 retire early

_____

5 walk out of a meeting

_____

6 interrupt in the middle of a presentation

_____

7 **Look at these proposed government measures and write the probable consequence of each one.**

The government is planning to:

0 introduce a road charging scheme for cars in big cities.
  This will reduce traffic congestion.

1 give working women extra money to pay for the cost of child care. _____

2 reduce the level of benefit payments to the unemployed. _____

3 increase income tax for top earners from 40% to 60%. _____

4 reduce taxes for companies with fewer than ten employees. _____

5 provide every primary school with a computer room. _____

6 subsidise rail transport for commuters.

_____

Pronunciation

8 English has a lot of vowel sounds, both long and short. One common mistake for learners of English is to shorten the long ones. Decide if the following words contain a long or short vowel sound and complete the table.

laid	food	slip
said	good	sleep
above	medium	include
move	medical	pudding
cloth	range	client
both	rang	clinic

long vowels	short vowels

9 Check your answers to exercise 8, then say the words aloud. If you exaggerate the length or shortness of each vowel, you will come close to the natural sound.

Relocation experiences

10 Read the description of a relocation advice service and complete it by writing one of the words from the box in each gap (1–8).

> grants   exempt   outgoing   premises   rental
> authority   property   move   estate

Derbyshire relocation services

We are a team funded by Derbyshire local (0) authority that provides business relocation services for both incoming and (1) _____ company personnel. Our packages include a wide range of services such as:

- orientation around the area

- assistance with finding business (2) _____ and moving house (purchase or (3) _____)

- help obtaining local government (4) _____

- advice on local schools.

We work with local commercial and residential (5) _____ agents, whether for buying or selling your (6) _____ . Our services have been designed for employees who are moving within the UK, but also for their company's own HR staff. Our aim is to help our clients (7) _____ as smoothly as possible. Our services are not free but are (8) _____ from tax.

11 Match each of the expressions (1–8) with a phrase that means the same (A–I).

0 stress-free	A relaxed
1 laid-back	B convenient
2 a carrot	C go for it
3 handy	D an opportunity not to be missed
4 have it both ways	E an incentive
5 too good to pass up	F be there at the beginning
6 give it a second thought	G without hassle
7 take the plunge	H enjoy the benefits with no disadvantages
8 get in on the ground floor	I consider before acting

12 Complete the sentences with the correct preposition.

0 I have a good working relationship with her.
1 It is a relationship based _____ trust.
2 She showed a lot of interest _____ our products.
3 He has a reputation _____ being a tough negotiator.
4 He has access _____ some excellent contacts in the Trade Ministry.
5 Chinese people love eating _____ at restaurants.
6 Don't worry _____ the time it takes to build a relationship.
7 You should find _____ if you qualify _____ a government grant.
8 She has invested heavily _____ the company in the last five years.
9 They have spent a lot of money _____ new equipment.

11.2 Effective writing

Remember!

- Be organised.
- Be to the point.
- Be appropriate.

1 Complete this proposal by using linking words or phrases to make it flow more naturally. Use some of the words in the box.

> although   unfortunately   as we see it   so
> in spite of   to sum up   indeed   ~~also~~   first of all
> for example   moreover

PROPOSAL TO REVIEW MARKETING STRATEGY

This proposal analyses our current marketing strategy and **(0)** *also* makes some key recommendations on how it can be improved.

(1) _____ , a little background: The company has always favoured a mass-market approach to advertising. **(2)** _____ , with the help of the RJP advertising agency, it has enjoyed great success with its campaigns. **(3)** _____ , their services are not cheap. **(4)** _____ , similar results could be achieved more economically by using targeted marketing.

Targeted marketing allows advertisers to reach particular groups of consumers more effectively. **(5)** _____ , we could use it to advertise our new training shoe line to millennials on social media. We also feel that a new marketing approach could help product development. **(6)** _____ , it could even lead to greater product innovation.

(7) _____ , we feel that **(8)** _____ a change in marketing strategy would require people to take time to adjust, in the long term the strategy would be hugely beneficial to the company.

2 Make these sentences from a report more concise by removing unnecessary words.

0 The aim of this report, and the purpose for it, is to evaluate, through careful examination, the current situation with our repair service offered for faulty goods.
The aim of this report is to evaluate our repair service for faulty goods.

1 In terms of price for a top of the range hairdryer, we consider that $150 is much too expensive for people to afford.

2 To sum up, I would like to conclude by saying that of the two options presented above, my preference would be to choose the second option since it represents a more cost-effective solution, and money is clearly an important consideration.

3 Put the underlined phrases in an internal email into a less formal style.

●●●

Dear Jim

I hope you are well. I **(0)** <u>apologise for</u> I'm sorry about the long delay in replying to your email. **(1)** <u>However,</u> I wanted to research your question thoroughly before **(2)** <u>providing you with an answer</u>.

You **(3)** <u>enquired whether</u> it was possible to extend the life of our standard mobile phone battery, **(4)** <u>since</u> you have received a **(5)** <u>significant number</u> of complaints about it. The answer is 'yes', but the solution may be expensive. We source our batteries from a Korean supplier which manufactures three different grades of battery. The ones **(6)** <u>which we purchase</u> are the cheapest in the range. **(7)** <u>It will come as no surprise that</u> they also have the shortest life.

If you **(8)** <u>wish</u> me to send you more technical details, **(9)** <u>please do not hesitate to</u> ask me.

11.3 Speaking Test: Part Two

1 Look at the topic below, chosen by a candidate in the Speaking Test, and the transcript of the presentation and discussion. Correct the mistakes the candidates made, using the examiner's notes.

Time Management
The importance of:
- organising your time efficiently
- prioritising tasks.

2 Imagine you are the examiner. Write two questions that you would like to ask the candidates about what they have said.

Do you think you manage your time effectively?
_____
_____
_____

---

0 singular / plural

Christine I'd like to say (**0**) some few words about time management. *[a]*

1 tense

A lot of people (**1**) are finding it very difficult to organise their time efficiently and I think that there are two simple rules you can follow that will help you.

2 verb form
3 modal verb

The first thing I recommend is planning and (**2**) make lists of the things that you (**3**) must to do each day, and then look at the list and see what is manageable and what is not.

4 preposition

Secondly, it's very important to prioritise the things (**4**) at your list to be sure that you are getting the important things done first. I

5 adverb / adjective

think that a lot of people go first to the things that are (**5**) easily to do rather than those which are really important and need doing.

6 tense

I think (**6**) I mentioned the main points. Do you have any questions Andrea?

7 gerund / infinitive
8 missing word
9 vocabulary
10 gerund / infinitive

Andrea Yes, I agree with you about the need (**7**) of prioritising. There is just one point I (**8**) would to add, which is that if you (**9**) do long lists of the things you have to do it can be quite alarming and the temptation is (**10**) doing the things which are quickest to do, so that you cross off the most items.

11 modal verb
12 preposition
13 word order

Christine Yes, that's right. You (**11**) must probably put a time next to each item according (**12**) on how long it's going to take. Or (**13**) even you can have two lists, one of short-term goals and one of long-term goals.

12.1   Crossing cultures

Globalisation

1 In the context of globalisation, think of a word that goes with each of the following.

0 merging *cultures*

1 _____ village

2 multinational _____

3 _____ barriers

4 cheap _____

5 _____ movement of capital

6 global _____

7 _____ countries

8 deregulated _____

2 Read the quotations in the speech bubbles and say who thinks globalisation:

0 is beneficial only for well-off people in developed countries.   *Jimmy Carter*

1 should be about more than just investing where you want to.   _____

2 will only be considered a success if it makes people better off in the long term.   _____

3 means that the free market determines the direction of world politics.   _____

4 means that companies can recruit better people.   _____

5 is just another term for expansion of American power.   _____

6 is good for the consumer.   _____

'Globalisation and free trade do spur economic growth, and they lead to lower prices on many goods.' Robert Reich

'If you're totally illiterate and living on one dollar a day, the benefits of globalisation never come to you.' Jimmy Carter

'The regime of globalisation promotes an unfettered marketplace as the dynamic instrument organising international relations.' William Greider

'Globalisation presumes sustained economic growth; otherwise, the process loses its economic benefits and political support.' Robert J Samuelson

'Globalisation has changed us into a company that searches the world, not just to sell or to source, but to find intellectual capital – the world's best talents and greatest ideas.' Jack Welch

'There is a growing consensus that globalisation must now be reshaped to reflect values broader than simply the freedom of capital.' John J Sweeney

'For when we talk about the spreading power and influence of globalisation, aren't we really referring to the spreading economic and military might of the US?' Fredric Jameson

Speculation

3 Complete this table of verb forms used to speculate about the past. Then write an example sentence for each form.

wish + _____

should + _____ + past participle

If + past perfect, _____ + *have* + past participle

could / might + *have* + _____

4 Write the following in order, from 99% certainty that it <u>was</u> the case to 99% certainty that it <u>wasn't</u>.

It might have been John who told them.
It must have been John who told them.
It can't have been John who told them.
It could have been John who told them.
It may have been John who told them.

_____ 99% **YES**
_____ 50%
_____ 50%
_____ 50%
_____ 99% **NO**

5 Write the correct form of the verb in brackets to complete each of these sentences.

0 I wish I *had known* (know) that before I spoke to her.

1 If I _____ (feel) more confident, I would have taken the risk.

2 You should _____ (ask) me. I would have said 'yes'.

3 If you had lost it, I _____ (be) furious.

4 I wish that I _____ (not / mention) that I was looking for another job.

5 I don't know why he's so late. I suppose he might _____ (forget).

6 I don't think anyone could _____ (predict) that this would happen.

6 Look at each situation and then complete the sentence speculating about it.

0 The management didn't really listen and so employees voted to strike.
The result might *have been different if the management had listened.* (be different if ...)

1 They were in such a hurry to launch the new product that they didn't test it properly for faults.
They wished _____ (do more tests)

2 They advertised the job internally and only got two applicants.
They could _____ (get a better response if ...)

3 He made the decision independently and then was surprised when everyone felt ignored.
He should _____ (consult more people)

4 She found that without a university education, her career progress was limited.
She wished _____ (go to university)

5 She sold her shares in France Telecom two months before the stock market crash.
If she _____ (keep her shares)

6 Both sides maintained their position and no agreement was reached.
If either side _____ (make a compromise)

7 They offered me a job and I refused. Since then, the company has been incredibly successful.
I should _____ (take the job)

8 They went bankrupt because they failed to invest when they needed to.
They could _____ (avoid bankruptcy if ...)

Pronunciation

7 Decide whether the letter 'g' in the following words is pronounced as a hard or soft sound; for example, *got* = hard 'g', *German* = soft 'g'. Complete the table.

> ~~merge~~ manager gentleman target
> colleague angel gesture region angle
> margin guest legal global

hard 'g'	soft 'g'
	merge

Cross-cultural communication

8 Write down two suggestions for the following:

0 things you can present to a business partner you are visiting
   a small gift OR your business card

1 ways to dress for a business meeting

_____

2 gestures used to greet someone you meet

_____

3 ways to address your business partner

_____

4 ways of talking to your business guest to make them feel relaxed.

_____

9 Read the passage and say what you think the ultimate gesture is.

The ultimate gesture

According to Roger G. Axtell, the 'ultimate gesture' carries certain welcome characteristics unlike any other single gesture.

First, this 'ultimate gesture' is known everywhere in the world. It is absolutely universal.

Second, it is rarely, if ever, misunderstood. Primitive tribes and world leaders alike know and use this gesture.

Third, scientists believe this particular gesture actually produces a beneficial physiological effect.

Fourth, as you travel around the world, this gesture may help you get out of the most difficult situations.

What is this singular signal, this miracle mien, this giant of all gestures?

10 Complete these sentences on behaviour in different countries by writing ONE word in each gap (1–9). The first letter has been given for you.

Body language around the world

China

The western custom of (**0**) shaking hands is the customary form of greeting, but often a (**1**) n _____ of the head is sufficient.

Far East

One thing all far eastern cultures have in (**2**) c _____ is a tendency to avoid direct eye (**3**) c _____ . Respect for authority and for one's elders is also a strong (**4**) f _____ of Asian culture. People in the Far East will also avoid (**5**) l _____ face or bringing shame on their social group.

Japan

Japanese are very polite people and yawning or blowing your nose in public is considered (**6**) r _____ .

Philippines

Filipinos may (**7**) g _____ one another with a quick lifting of the eyebrows.

Korea

Having first- (**8**) h _____ experience of Korean negotiating style is very important, because your style may prove more important than the price.

America

(**9**) A _____ of personal space is important. It is impolite to stand closer than 75 cm to someone.

12.2 Social English

Small talk

1 Match each of the expressions 0–8 with the phrase that is closest in meaning from A–I.

0 It's not important.	A Would you like a lift?
1 That would be great.	B Don't worry.
2 Can I help you?	C I don't want to put you out.
3 Please do.	D Can I give you a hand?
4 That is a nice offer.	E Do you mind if I ...?
5 You're welcome.	F That's very kind of you.
6 Please don't trouble yourself.	G Not at all.
7 Is it OK for me to ...?	H I'd love to.
8 Can I take you in my car?	I Go ahead.

2 Respond to each of these statements / questions with a short response

0 Hi, how are you?
   Fine, thanks. And you?

1 How do you do? I'm Jane Moor.

   _____

2 I'm so sorry to be late.

   _____

3 Thank you for all your help.

   _____

4 Lovely weather, isn't it?

   _____

5 How was your trip?

   _____

6 Can I give you a hand with that suitcase?

   _____

7 You're looking well.

   _____

8 Would you like to go for a drink after work?

   _____

9 Can I just answer the phone?

   _____

10 Do you mind if I smoke?

   _____

3 Correct the underlined words in this conversation.

Qiu Qing Hello. I hope you (**0**) <u>didn't</u> *haven't* been waiting long.

Paul No. It's OK. I brought some work with me. How are you?

Qiu Qing I'm very (**1**) <u>fine</u> _____ , thank you. And you?

Paul Quite busy these days. But things are going well.

Qiu Qing I'm glad (**2**) <u>hearing</u> _____ that.

Paul Would you like a coffee?

Qiu Qing Yes, that (**3**) <u>is</u> _____ great. But I don't want to put you (**4**) <u>off</u> _____ .

Paul It's no trouble. But it's instant, I'm afraid.

Qiu Qing Don't (**5**) <u>be troubled</u> _____ . I prefer instant.

Paul Sorry, that's my phone ringing. Do you mind if I take the call?

Qiu Qing No, of course not. Please (**6**) <u>get forward</u> _____ . I'm not (**7**) <u>on</u> _____ a hurry.

Paul Sorry about that. So, what about the contract? Do you think Thompson will sign?

Qiu Qing Well, I hope (**8**) <u>it</u> _____ , but I am beginning to doubt (**9**) <u>so</u> _____ . I have another meeting with them next week.

Paul Is there anything I can do to help?

Qiu Qing That's kind (**10**) <u>to</u> _____ you, but I think it's easier for me to deal with the Chinese representative.

Paul Whatever you prefer.

12.3 Reading Test: Part Five and Part Six

1 Do Part Five of the Reading Test. Give yourself ten minutes to complete the task.

- Read this article about Iceland's energy resources.
- Write ONE word in each gap (1–10).
- There is an example at the beginning (0).

If there is a paradise for environmentalists, Iceland must be (0) ....it.... . It is the world's most energy-efficient country, with 70% of its needs covered by domestically produced renewables. The volcanic island and (1) .... 300,000 inhabitants are blessed with natural hot springs. All (2) .... the island's electricity is produced cleanly – 84% through hydropower, while the rest comes from geothermal energy, using the heat from the earth.

Fossil fuels are used only for transport, but (3) .... here Iceland is determined to get rid of them completely. In 1998, the government decided to replace oil and gas (4) .... hydrogen as soon as possible. Three years ago, it opened the world's first hydrogen station and started a trial of three buses powered by hydrogen.

But it was (5) .... always like this. Iceland used to be a poor country that (6) .... to rely on imports of fossil fuels for everything. That (7) .... until the 1973 oil shock, when OPEC countries quadrupled prices. At that point Iceland started converting houses to geothermal heating, which is very cheap and costs less (8) .... fossil fuels.

There have been attempts to export Iceland's green riches abroad. Studies have been made on trying to send electricity through cables to Scotland, but (9) .... the moment it's not economical. If energy prices continue to go up and the price of the technology comes down, (10) .... something could be done about it. If exploited to the full, it is thought the energy could supply all of the electricity of a country the size of Scotland.

2 Do Part Six of the Reading Test. Give yourself ten minutes to complete the task.

- In most of the lines there is one extra word. It is either grammatically incorrect or does not fit in with the sense of the text. Some lines, however, are correct.
- If a line is correct, write CORRECT next to it.
- If there is an extra word, write the extra word next to it.

0	Economic 'globalisation' is a historical and process, the result of	......and......
00	human innovation and technological progress. It refers to the increasing	CORRECT
1	integration of economies around the world, particularly through trade	....
2	and financial flows. The term sometimes can also refers to the movement of	....
3	people (labour) and knowledge (technology) across international borders.	....
4	There are also with broader cultural, political and environmental dimensions	....
5	to globalisation. At its most basic, there is not nothing mysterious about	....
6	globalisation. The term has come into common usage since the 1980s,	....
7	reflecting technological advances that have made it more easier and quicker	....
8	to complete international transactions – both trade and financial flows.	....
9	It refers on to an extension beyond national borders of the same market forces	....
10	that have been operated for centuries at all levels of human economic activity	....
11	– village markets, urban industries, or financial centres. Markets promote	....
12	efficiency by allowing people and economies to focus on that what they do best.	....

Answer key

MODULE 1

1.1
Working life

1
1 educated	2 left	3 applied
4 trained	5 set up	6 joined
7 graduated	8 moved	9 worked
10 recruited	11 retired	

2 1 unemployment 2 trainees (*people who receive training*) 3 recruitment 4 pay (= *salary; payment means a single instance* eg *'please make your payment by credit card'*) 5 promotion 6 applications (*applicants are the people who apply*) 7 retirement 8 training

3 1 There's no point / It's useless + gerund 2 I plan / I aim + infinitive 3 I am thinking of / I am considering + gerund 4 I am prepared / I am happy + infinitive 5 I adore / I am keen on + gerund 6 I wasn't able / I failed + infinitive

4
1 I'm not used to **driving on the left**.
2 She is good at **managing people**.
3 I plan **to leave at the end of the year**.
4 Did you manage **to contact Jane**?
5 She is reluctant **to increase the prices**.
6 Did you have any difficulty **downloading the software**?
7 Does the job involve **speaking French**?
8 When do you expect **to arrive approximately**?
9 What do you think about **going to the cinema**?
10 Please avoid **calling between 10 and 12**.
11 The flights are full. Would you consider **taking the train**?
12 It's not worth **flying business class**.

5 In words of two syllables the stress falls on the first syllable if the word is a noun, on the second syllable if the word is a verb

6 **ba**ckground su**pply** **con**tract **stu**dent pro**mote** in**vol**ve re**tain** **col**lege at**tend** **sta**tus

7 pre**sent** verb per**mit** verb **ob**ject noun **in**crease noun **con**flict noun **con**test noun ex**port** verb in**sult** verb

8
0 A (*we are looking for bright and capable young graduates*)
1 B (*independent and responsible*)
2 B (*regardless of the candidate's sex, religion or ethnic background*)
3 C (*Please supply character references*)
4 B (*master's degree, 10 years' nursing experience* etc.)
5 A (*No direct experience is necessary*)
6 C (*voted 'most dynamic newcomer'*)
7 A (*Excellent career prospects*)

1.2
Asking and answering questions

1
1 First of all, Dr Wolf, can you tell me why this price rise is necessary?
2 Obviously, it's not something we wanted to do. It has been forced on us by higher oil prices.
3 But you don't actually produce much of your electricity from burning oil, do you?
4 No, but the price of gas is linked to the price of oil and we do burn a lot of gas.
5 But even if gas has gone up, how can you justify these prices when you have just announced record profits?
6 These new prices are necessary to protect our future profits, not our past profits.
7 Oh, I see. So you'll be making just as much money out of your customers this year, will you?
8 In fact, our profits this year will be used to fund a very expensive investment programme in our network.
9 And finally, do you know why other companies haven't increased their prices by the same amount?
10 I can't speak for others, but I would be surprised if they didn't increase them in the near future.

2
1 Do you actually produce much of your electricity from burning oil?
2 Will you be making just as much money out of your customers this year?
3 Why haven't other companies increased their prices by the same amount?

3
1 You are quite inexperienced, aren't you?
2 How much sales experience do you have?
3 Do you think you have the necessary skills for the job?
4 You have done this kind of work before, haven't you? / You haven't done this kind of work before, have you?
5 Would you like a coffee?
6 You don't live in London, do you?
7 Why did you leave your last job?
8 Can you tell me why you find this job attractive?

1.3
Reading Test: Part One

1 0 D (*people entering the workforce are very poorly equipped to deal with the demands of working life*)

1 E (*we, the older generation, must accept that these are the values of today*)

2 A (*they think less about work and more about leisure time*)

3 C (*it doesn't necessarily follow that they are less committed to their jobs*)

4 E (*a fear of being poor*)

5 B (*Employees have much less loyalty to their employers these days*)

6 D (*when they are faced with the prospect of learning more on the job and serving their time to gain this necessary experience, they become frustrated*)

7 B (*they need this flexibility*)

MODULE 2

2.1
Growing the company

1 1 warehouse   2 subsidiary   3 plant
4 headquarters   5 division

2 British bank fears **takeover** by cash-rich Spanish giant
Car plant closes: 800 **laid off**
Keltel to **sell off** failing Internet business
BP and Shell **merge** to form world's largest oil company
Deanly shares will **go public** next year
Administrators called in as Lanco **goes bankrupt**
Chemico **expands** its European operations by buying Toxico

3

Verb	Noun
expand	expansion
develop	**development**
merge	**merger**
acquire	**acquisition**
grow	**growth**
innovate	innovation
solve	solution
classify	classification
evolve	evolution
tend	tendency

4 a) The stress always falls on the syllable before *-ion*.
b) In other words of three or more syllables the stress often falls on the third from last syllable.

5 **ban**kruptcy evo**lu**tion di**vi**sion sub**si**diary **stra**tegy distri**bu**tion sig**ni**ficant compe**ti**tion com**pe**titive phi**lo**sophy

6

Present	Past	Past participle
begin	**began**	begun
become	became	**become**
lose	lost	**lost**
buy	**bought**	**bought**
put	**put**	put
rise	**rose**	risen
fall	fell	**fallen**
feel	**felt**	**felt**
spend	spent	**spent**
find	**found**	found
found	**founded**	**founded**

7 1 C   2 F   3 B   4 G   5 E   6 D

8 1 Even though revenue was down over the course of the year, our profit margins <u>improved</u>. ✓

2 In April, we ~~had begun~~ work on a bus terminal in Shanghai. **began**

3 In Shanghai we used the same design that we ~~used to use~~ in Beijing a year earlier. **had used**

4 Because many existing projects <u>were coming</u> to an end, we made it a priority to look for new business. ✓ (*we could also say here 'had come to an end'*)

5 In May, a new head of International Business ~~has been~~ appointed. **was**

6 We found that we ~~wasted~~ a lot of time in the planning stages. **were wasting / had wasted**

7 The official opening <u>was</u> attended by the president of Iran. ✓

8 Our R & D department ~~was working~~ on a new high speed railway which will be launched next year. **has been working**

9

Employees — Stakeholders — eg Customers
Shareholders — Suppliers
Local community

10 1 I am very **involved** in the development of new products.

2 Customers are generally very **satisfied** with the service they get. (*something is 'satisfactory', people are 'satisfied'*)

3 We have a very **hierarchichal** structure, with about 15 levels from top to bottom.

4 It's a very **innovative** company which empowers individuals.

5 I am consulted both on everyday matters and also on more **strategic** decisions.

11 6 At Google the emphasis is on **informality**.

7 Like most banks, our culture is influenced by the amount of **bureaucracy**.

8 The most important thing for employees is to have **consistency**; not constant change.

9 In advertising, the main thing is to bring out employees' natural **creativity**.

10 **Recognition** can be financial or simply a few words of praise.

12 1 balance 2 reward 3 empowered
4 recognised 5 mutual 6 satisfaction
7 welfare 8 clear 9 retention

2.2
Presenting facts

1 0 D 1 E 2 I 3 A 4 H 5 F 6 C 7 B 8 G

2 1 From 2 in 3 before 4 for 5 by 6 to 7 over
8 for 9 over 10 also

3 1 ... to present our reasons **to you** ... (OR ... to **present our** ...)

2 I'm going to describe **to** you the development ... (OR ... to **describe the** development ...)

3 And I'd like to **ask you** this question ...

4 Can anyone tell **me** why we ... (OR Can anyone **say** why we ...)

5 When I have explained the reasons **to** you ... (OR ... **explained the** reasons ...)

6 The next graph **shows you** how we ... (OR ... **shows** how we ...)

4 Students' own answers.

2.3
Speaking Test: Part One

1 1 **Actually**, it's German.

2 Yes but, **for me**, money is not the important thing.

3 **I don't see it that way**. I think it is a very risky strategy.

4 **On the whole**, that's true, but there are opportunities.

5 **Not really**. It tends to be less dynamic.

6 **I doubt it**. It's only a two-year contract.

7 **I agree**. It affects your whole career.

2 1 E 2 F 3 A 4 B 5 D

3 1 **Examiner** What does your job involve exactly?
Candidate I am responsible **for** searching the press **every day** / **each day** for articles about our company.

2 **Examiner** Will you continue to work there at the end of your apprenticeship?
Candidate Yes, I hope **so**. But maybe I **will have to** apply for a job with another company.

3 **Examiner** And what do you hope to be doing ten years from now?
Candidate My ambition is **to work** in the marketing field, because that is what I **specialise** in.

4 **Examiner** Do you think it's OK for pharmaceutical companies to advertise medicines?
Candidate It depends **on** what kind of product they are advertising. In my **view** / **opinion**, it's fine to advertise if you are honest about the benefits.

5 **Examiner** But perhaps that's not always the case?
Candidate I **agree** with you that some companies overstate benefits, but **on the whole** they are very responsible.

MODULE 3
3.1
Communication at work

1 1 receiving 2 issuing / putting out 3 attending
4 taking 5 makes / gives 6 produce / publish
7 putting / posting 8 running / launching
9 circulating / sending out

2
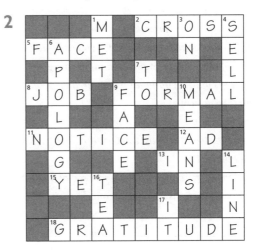

3 1 I **do** apologise for the delay.

2 If you **would** be kind enough to give me your mobile number, I'll call you back in a few minutes.

3 I **do** understand your worries.

4 **Would** 9am be a convenient time?

5 I**'ll** get back to you as soon as I can.

6 **Can** I be of any more assistance?

7 You **may** call me on this number whenever you like.

5 1 G 2 F 3 H 4 B 5 E 6 A 7 D

6
1 promise and undertake **to do something**
2 urge and encourage **someone to do something**
3 suggest and propose **doing** or **that someone do something**
4 persuade and convince **someone to do something**
5 dissuade and discourage **someone from doing something**
6 ask and invite **someone to do something**
7 criticise and blame **someone for doing something**

7
1 The finance minister promised **to simplify the tax system and to reduce the burden of tax on companies.**
2 The chairman urged **investors to be patient** …
3 A source close to the management suggested **relaunching the product in a year or so.**
4 Hamilton praised **his team for working hard** …
5 Fredericks denied **showing favouritism to his son** …
6 The industry watchdog criticised **Degas for putting unfair pressure on customers.**
7 The spokeswoman discouraged **consumers from buying dairy products from France until more was known about the disease.**
8 The head of the airline threatened **to drop prices too, if the competition dropped theirs** …

8
0 C   (*share the best and most interesting content … that genuinely educate visitors*)
1 D   (*the whole object of the exercise … is to bring people … into the sales pipeline*)
2 C, E (C: *such posts will provoke and encourage meaningful conversations*; E: *if … you can build a bank of coherent, engaging and informative messages with an individual flavour, then people will take notice*)
3 D   (*might send users … to a competitor.*)
4 C   (*share the best and most interesting content … So … you put up links*)
5 A   (*No business … can afford to ignore social media*)
6 A, B (A: *Social media is a two-way conversation*; B: *People in social media spaces … want a … conversation that engages them and that they would like to engage others in*)
7 B   (*People in social media spaces don't want to be shouted at or bombarded with sales messages.*)
8 E   (*there lies the real challenge … if, over time, you can build a bank of coherent, engaging and informative messages with an individual flavour, then people will take notice*)

3.2
Email exchange

1 Dear Didier
(**0**) Thanks for offering to (**1**) **help** me with the Blane report. The chairman specifically (**2**) **suggested that I** compile it and (**3**) **so** I (**4**) **don't** feel I (**5**) **can** accept your kind offer. (**6**) **But** (**7**) **please** send me any relevant information that might help me with it. (**8**) **Do** call me if you (**9**) **would like** to discuss it (**10**) **more**.
Kind regards
Jean

2 Dear Ms Doyle
(**0**) Thank you for your email. (**1**) **I apologise** for the delay in sending you the T-shirt that you ordered.
(**2**) **Currently**, we (**3**) **do not** have the medium size you asked for in stock. We hope to have delivery of these on Friday. (**4**) **As soon as** they arrive, (**5**) **I will** (**6**) **send** one out to you by first class post. Or, if (**7**) **you would prefer**, I can send you either a small or large T-shirt of the same design immediately. If this is the case, (**8**) **I would be grateful** (**9**) **if you could contact me** and let me know.
(**10**) **In the meantime**, I will try to get the medium size in as soon as possible.
(**11**) **My apologies** once again.
(**12**) **Yours sincerely**
Gareth Evans

3
1 consequently	2 nevertheless
3 In the meantime	4 Moreover
5 Following	6 However
7 Besides	8 Since

3.3
Listening Test: Part One

1
1 A year or date, eg *1996*
2 Qualities / skills, eg *presentation skills*
3 An adverb, eg *well, badly*
4 A period, eg *3 weeks*
5 An adjective, eg *confident, relaxed*
6 A verb phrase, eg *feel relaxed / listen*
7 Qualities, eg *natural abilities*
8 A plural noun, eg *meetings / business relationships*
9 A plural noun, eg *people / situations*
10 An adjective, eg *uncomfortable*
11 A training tool, eg *simulations*
12 Type of literature, eg *leaflet, brochure*

2 1 False 2 False 3 True 4 True 5 False

MODULE 4

4.1

The art of selling

1
1 H emotional benefits
2 G buying signal
3 J unique selling point
4 F payment terms
5 E sales technique
6 B competitive advantage
7 K price competition
8 A decision maker
9 I added value
10 D after-sales service

2
1 word of mouth
2 sponsorship
3 point of sale promotion
4 billboards
5 direct mail (or mailing)
6 viral marketing

3
1 C pushing   2 A buying   3 C close
4 B persuade   5 C need   6 B strategy

4
1 launched   2 have collected
3 have circulated   4 has been
5 will have decided 6 tend
7 is looking   8 will write

5
1 Up to now   2 In the last decade
3 Sooner or later 4 Currently
5 In the past   6 since I was born

6
1 Correct
2 Incorrect (*raised everyone's hopes*)
3 Correct
4 Incorrect (*has declined*)
5 Correct
6 Correct
7 Incorrect (*raise, increase,* etc)
8 Incorrect (*reducing / lowering / dropping the price*)

7
1 placing   2 delivery   3 stock
4 commission   5 mark   6 volume
7 chain   8 promotional

8
increased /t/   changed /d/
picked /t/   ended /ɪd/
plummeted /ɪd/   reached /t/
recovered /d/   decreased /t/
fluctuated /ɪd/   rocketed /ɪd/
stayed /d/   levelled /d/
developed /t/   recorded /ɪd/
dropped /t/

9
1 fluctuated wildly
2 reached a peak
3 continued on an upward trend with some fluctuations
4 remained relatively stable
5 recovered slightly
6 increased steadily
7 developed in a similar way
8 diverged significantly

4.2

Presenting figures

1
1 at   2 in   3 from   4 In / By
5 to   6 of   7 with   8 into / to
9 by   10 At

2
1 I'm going to present
2 If we look at the first graph
3 As you can see
4 The second graph shows
5 Comparing the two
6 In conclusion
7 Thanks for your attention
8 Now if there are any questions

3
1 It resulted **in a lot of people cancelling their holidays.**
2 It led **to a lot of people cancelling their holidays.**
3 It meant **that a lot of people cancelled their holidays.**
4 It was on account **of their (having) very talented software designers.**
5 It was thanks **to some very talented software designers.**
6 It had a lot to do **with their (having) very talented software designers.**

4.3

Writing Test: Part One

1
0 **True** – use the rubric to help you write a brief introduction to what you are going to describe.
1 **False** – some will be unavoidable, but try to rephrase the question in your own words.
2 **True**
3 **False** – just describe the general development.
4 **True** – this can either be a general comment at the beginning or conclusion at the end.
5 **False** – you only need to comment on the facts presented; if reasons are obvious then you can give them.
6 **False** – you must show that you have understood the information presented.

2 **Model answer:**

The graph shows the production levels achieved by factories in three different locations over the period 2012 to 2017. Overall, we can see that, although the three factories vary in size and production capacity, the output at all the sites has followed a similar upward trend.

In Guangzhou, the largest of the three, output rose from 7.6 million to 12 million units over the period in question, the best growth in percentage terms. In Timisoara, production rose by about 35% over the same period, despite a slight fall recorded in 2014. In Leeds, output also grew year on year but increased more slowly, from 7 million in 2012 to 8.5 million in 2017.

In conclusion we can observe that production at all three sites has shown a healthy level of growth, reflecting an increased demand for the company's products.

MODULE 5

5.1

Money and finance

1
1 borrowed	2 wasted	3 made	4 make
5 charge	6 saved	7 is worth	8 spent
9 owe	10 off		

2 **lend, owe, invoice, charge** someone money <u>for</u> something
spend, bet, save, waste money <u>on</u> something

3
1 take	2 in	3 much	4 on
5 turnover	6 made	7 security	8 worth
9 owe	10 accounts		

5
1 than	2 much	3 by	4 as, as
5 more	6 less		

6

Adjective (or adverb)	Comparative form	Superlative form
clever	*cleverer*	*the cleverest*
good	**better**	the best
quickly	**more quickly***	**the most quickly**
tiring	**more tiring**	the most tiring
bad	worse	**the worst**
well (adverb)	**better**	**the best**
far	**further / farther**	**the furthest / the farthest**
little	**less**	the least
much	more	**the most**

* You will sometimes hear people say '*she works quicker than him*' or '*he ran the quickest of all of them*'.

7
1 Life expectancy in Japan **is much higher than in** Kenya.
2 Japan **has a slightly bigger** population than Mexico.
3 Kenya's inflation rate is **very similar to** Russia's.
4 The number of Internet users in Mexico **is much higher than in** France.
5 Egypt's GDP **is not nearly as high as** Russia's.
6 China and Mexico have **exactly the same** life expectancy.
7 Japan **has a very high number of** Internet users compared to its total population.
8 The USA **is by far the richest** country in the table.
9 Inflation in Egypt is **much greater than in** other countries.
10 France's unemployment rate is **three times higher than** Japan's.

8
1 liabilities	2 equity	3 loss	4 turnover
5 costs	6 gross	7 net	8 bottom
9 creditors	10 investments		

9 1 E   2 B   3 G   4 A   5 D   6 H

10 **Possible answers:**
material costs   administrative costs   distribution costs
labour costs   research and development costs
finance costs   fixed costs   direct costs   rent
advertising expenditure   maintenance costs
capital expenditure

5.2

Discussing options

1 **Possible answers:**
1 Ask for someone's opinion
  What's your view / opinion of …? or *What do you think?*
2 Make a suggestion
  I would recommend doing … or *We could try doing …*
3 State a preference
  For me, the best thing would be to …
4 Agree with someone
  I agree with you.
5 Disagree politely
  I see what you're saying, but wouldn't it be better to …
6 Suggest an alternative course of action
  Instead of doing …, we should …

2
1 G I think it would be better to expand slowly.
2 B I have some reservations about entering the Chinese market.
3 A We shouldn't rush into making a decision.
4 I The advantage of Hungary is that it's near.
5 H We would be better off concentrating on Europe.

6 E I think China represents the best opportunity.

7 F I suggest that we wait a year.

8 D Personally, I would go for the eastern European market.

3 **MD** I wanted to ask your advice about the rise in steel prices.

DD What do you want to know exactly?

MD Well, what do you suggest that we do about it?

DD As I see it, we've got two options. We could absorb the cost or pass it on to our customers.

MD And which of those two do you recommend?

DD I'd recommend absorbing the cost for now. The price of steel may come down again.

MD My only reservation about that is that it will hurt our profit margins.

DD Maybe, in the short term, but if we were to pass the cost on, we might lose customers.

MD I see what you're saying, but wouldn't it be better to lose a few than to be unprofitable?

DD That's the decision you have to make, but you've heard my opinion now.

5.3

Listening Test: Part Two

1

TASK ONE – SECTOR	TASK TWO – FINANCIAL PROBLEM
1 E education	1 F being paid late
2 B clothes retail	2 C expensive premises
3 A car repair	3 G loans to repay
4 H mail order firm	4 E high cost of advertising
5 F property / real estate	5 B investment risk

MODULE 6

6.1

Purchasing power

1 1 C 2 D 3 B 4 B 5 A 6 C 7 D 8 A 9 C
10 C

2 1 extension 2 seasonal 3 squeezing 4 raw
5 exclusive 6 pass 7 terms 8 feedback

3 1 Launches *a call for tender*, giving the *technical specifications*

2 *Bids for / tenders for* the contract

3 Evaluates the *bids / offers*; makes a shortlist

4 *Negotiates* the details

5 *Awards* the contract to a supplier

6 *Wins / loses* the contract

4 1 Any company **which wishes** to be considered must submit their bid by 20 April.

2 Bids **which have been / are submitted** after that date will not be considered.

3 Anyone **who gives** inaccurate information will be disqualified.

4 Prices **which have been / are quoted** in this initial bid will be treated as negotiable.

5 Anyone **questioning** the terms should contact our contracts office.

6 Companies **owned** by a larger group or parent company must declare this fact.

7 Suppliers **failing to** fulfil all the conditions need not apply.

8 The decision **made** on 14 May will be final.

5 1 have submitted

2 will be

3 tendered

4 did

5 have not done

6 are continuing / will continue

6 1 E 2 B 3 D 4 F 5 C

7 **Possible answer:**

Dear Mr James

I am writing to express my deep concern and anger about the fact that your team of builders have recently left the site of our offices in Portland Street with a lot of work unfinished, saying that they had been called to another job!

As you know, we contracted your company last November to fully rewire our offices and put up new partitioning. Work began in February and seemed to be progressing well. The wiring was fitted quickly and the partitioning also went up easily.

However, the job is by no means finished. Some of the new wiring is still exposed and the partitioning is not properly secured. Both these things represent a real health and safety hazard: someone could get electrocuted or fall through a wall. The consequence is that I have had to order some of the staff to work from home, while the remainder are squeezed into a small space not affected by your work.

This situation is not tolerable. It is costing our company valuable time and money. Unless your team return immediately, I will be forced to employ another building firm to come in and finish the job that you started. Their fees will be charged to you, or rather, will be deducted from your invoice, when it arrives.

I am sorry to give such an ultimatum, but the circumstances leave me no other choice. I look forward to hearing from you very soon.

Yours sincerely

8 1 <u>wor</u>k   w<u>a</u>lk   <u>lear</u>n

Both contain the sound /ɜː/ as in *were*; *walk* has the sound /ɔː/ as in *door*

2 l<u>aw</u>yer   l<u>au</u>nch   l<u>aw</u>

Both contain the sound /ɔː/ as in *door*; *lawyer* has the sound /ɔɪ/ as in *boy*

3 sp<u>e</u>cial   l<u>e</u>gal   <u>pre</u>sent

Both contain the sound /e/; *legal* has the sound /iː/ as in *keep*

4 <u>a</u>gent   <u>fai</u>lure   chat

Both contain the sound /eɪ/ as in *say*; *chat* has the sound /æ/ as in *cat*

5 m<u>o</u>nth   h<u>o</u>nest   fr<u>o</u>nt

Both contain the sound /ʌ/ as in *cup*; *honest* has the sound /ɒ/ as in *hot*

6.2
Telephoning

1 1 F   2 D   3 B   4 G   5 A   6 C

2 **Possible answers:**

1 His line is engaged. Would you like to hold?
No, that's OK. I'll **call back later**.

2 Can I give you the address?
Sure. One minute, I'll **just get a pen**.

3 Can I speak to someone in technical support?
One moment, I'll **put you through**.

4 Is the correct figure 7.8 or 8.7?
Hang on, I'll **check**.

5 I need the information urgently.
OK. I'll **send it to you immediately**.

6 Please tell Kevin that I will meet him outside 210 Regent Street at 10.30.
OK. I'll **give him the message**.

7 Do you have the information to hand?
No, but I'll **get back to you as soon as I can**.

8 So, 6 o'clock tomorrow at the Red Lion pub in George Street.
Great. I'll **look forward to it / seeing you then**.

3 **Possible answers:**

1 Hang on, please. I'll see if he's free.

2 Can I tell him who's calling?

3 Thank you, Mrs Jordan. I'll just put you through.

4 Hello. Fernandez speaking. How can I help you?

5 I'm from Mcmillion Publishers. I'm just calling to ask if you can make it to the book launch this evening.

6 I'll just check my diary. I'm afraid I'm already busy this evening.

7 Don't worry. It'll be repeated on 12 May. Does that suit you any better?

8 Perhaps. I'll have to get back to you on that.

9 OK. I'll look forward to hearing from you.

6.3
Writing Test: Part Two

1 Register: B
Tone: B
Content: C

2 1 experienced   2 As   3 result
4 order   5 willing / happy   6 hearing
7 from   8 sincerely

3 **Model answer:**

Dear Mr Opik

I apologise for missing your recent call concerning your new pool. I was also sorry and surprised to hear that you have experienced problems with it so soon.

As you will recall, when we originally discussed the question of heaters, I presented to you various options. Some were smaller heaters; others were more powerful. Clearly, different people have different tastes in how warm they would like their swimming pool to be. Consequently, at the time, I advised you to buy one that you thought would be best for you. You chose a smaller, less expensive one. I am sorry that you are now regretting that choice. As a result of this, we feel that it is not our responsibility to compensate you for a new heater. However, I do sympathise with your situation and in order to resolve this problem, I suggest that you ask the manufacturer for an exchange for a bigger heater. Generally, they are quite good about this sort of thing and should give you a full refund on the original heater.

If you like, I would be very willing to come and give my advice on which heater I personally would put in. This visit and advice would be free of charge.

I hope you find this solution acceptable and look forward to hearing from you.

Yours sincerely
Selma Chakrabati

MODULE 7
7.1
Managing people

1 1 B   2 A   3 G   4 D   5 I   6 J   7 C   8 K   9 F   10 H

2 1 get <u>my</u> hands dirty

2 get on with

3 <u>puts</u> people on the spot

4 <u>spreads</u> <u>himself</u> very thin

5 take <u>that</u> on board

6 cut corners

7 bite off more than you can chew

8 open a can of worms

3
1 different: /kæn/ /kɑːnt/
2 same: /bɔːd/
3 different: /fɜːst/ /fɑːst/
4 different: /liːd/ (or /led/) /laɪd/
5 same: /piːs/
6 same: /weɪt/
7 different: /wɒnt/ /wəʊnt/

4
1 Actually, I did an MBA **to avoid having** to look for a job immediately.
2 My main motivation was **just to understand** business better.
3 I wanted to do an MBA **in order to meet** people from different backgrounds.
4 I waited until I was 33 to do my MBA **so that I would get** the maximum benefit from it.
5 I did the MBA just **in case it was** useful in later life.
6 I was sent on an MBA by my insecure boss **to prevent me from taking** over his job!

5 Possible answers:
1 I am going to **read a lot more** to expand my vocabulary.
2 I am going to **listen to native speakers whenever possible** in order to improve my pronunciation.
3 I am going to **get some interview coaching** in case I am asked to speak English at a job interview.
4 I am going to make a list of my most common mistakes to avoid **making the same mistakes again and again**.
5 I am going to read more business magazines in order **to increase my knowledge of business matters**.
6 I am going to watch more English TV so that **I can understand fast native speech better**.

6
1 She rarely keeps anyone waiting.
2 He performs best under pressure.
3 He is never at his desk.
4 If you want something done properly, do it yourself.
5 I was completely exhausted after the trip.
6 Please send me an update at this address every Monday.
7 They will move their headquarters to Shanghai next month.

7
1 *Almost half considered ... getting rid of around 5% of the workforce each year – would actually be a positive measure.*
2 *... surveys of employees show that only 18% feel confident that their employer will look after them ... Around a third ... looking to leave their current job ... 51% indicate that they are 'not engaged' in their work ...*
3 *It's difficult to escape the conclusion that the culprit of all this is poor management.*
4 *... the best and worst-performing employees are identified. ... Fortunately, this practice is now in decline ...*
5 *... known as 'bottom-slicing' ... the thinking behind it – that the best way to improve performance is simply to start with a new employee ...*
6 *The answer to increased employee engagement ... managers need to put the measuring tools away and talk more to their employees ...*

8 1A 2A 3C 4D 5A 6B

7.2
Report writing

1 *All these points are important, but if you fail to observe those marked ++ you risk not passing this part of the exam.*

Answer all the points you have been asked to address accurately.   ++

Begin with a clear introduction of the aims of the report.   +

End with a definite conclusion and recommendation.   ++

Use sub-headings and bullet points to make the report clearer.   +

Be consistent in your arguments and connect your ideas with linking expressions.   ++

Use language naturally, appropriately and with a minimum of errors.   ++

Use sophisticated vocabulary and grammatical structure.   +

Organise the report so that it is clear which point is being addressed.   ++

2

0	to present	*'The aim is' + infinitive*
1	choice	*Verb 'to choose'; noun 'a choice'*
2	initial	*Adjective needed to describe the noun*
3	most	*Superlative to compare three things; 'more' is used when comparing two things*
4	at	*at a cost*
5	powerful	*The suffix 'ful' has a single 'l'*
6	a	*it is one of many bargains*
7	to get	*'It is difficult' + infinitive*
8	Another	*'The other' or 'another'; never 'the another'*
9	All	*'Every' is singular, ' all' is plural*
10	guarantees	*Spelling 'gua'*
11	which	*'that' is only used in defining relative clauses, eg 'the car that I rented.'*
12	purchasing	*'recommend' + gerund*
13	no	*'It has no ...' or 'It doesn't have any ...'*
14	could	*could = might = perhaps it will be; 'can' cannot be used to speculate in this way*
15	in	*in the long run.*

3 1 Although   2 On the whole   3 However   4 since   5 Indeed

7.3

Reading Test: Part Two

1   1 G   2 D   3 A   4 E   5 F   6 H

MODULE 8

8.1

Being responsible

1   1 Another letter to the newspaper about the waste of energy by large corporations.
2 For having shelves which are open and therefore need more energy to keep food cold.
3 It is much too cheap for people to be conscious of the need to save it.
4 In spite of how the younger generation appears to advocate environmental friendliness.
5 He is pessimistic and holds out little hope for the future.

2   1 campaign against   2 single out
3 present comfort and convenience

3   **Possible answers:**

Waste:	They can use less packaging, especially plastic containers and wrapping.
Transport:	They can use lorries / trucks that run on greener fuel.
	They can try to minimise the distance between warehouses and stores.
Energy:	They can switch off lights when they are not needed.
	They can encourage employees to avoid leaving electronics in 'standby' mode.
	They can buy green energy or install generation facilities onsite, like wind turbines or solar panels.
Suppliers:	They can trade more with fair-trade suppliers.
	They can buy more local produce in order to reduce food miles.

4   1 smog
2 extinction
3 drought
4 leak
5 flooding

5   1 Uromin shares increased **by** $1.2 **over** the six-month period.
2 Formetal shares stayed **at** the same level **for** three months.
3 **On** average both shares showed a rise **of** 50%.
4 Formetal shares climbed **to** $5.4 **by** the end of June.
5 Uromin shares reached a peak **of** $3.7 **in** May.

6   1 asking   2 to change   3 to establish
4 worrying   5 taking   6 to have
7 paying   8 beginning

7   to be committed / to get used / to look forward / to object + **to** do**ing** something OR **to** something

8   **Possible answers:**
1 You should knock before entering.
2 You mustn't take photographs in the main hall.
3 You must be authorised to enter this area.
4 You don't have to present a badge if you are a member of staff / you must present a badge unless you are a member of staff.
5 You should register here.
6 You may take / help yourself to a catalogue.

9   1 F   being accountable to the outside world for your actions
2 I   considering the welfare of your employees
3 G   taking account of the impact of your actions
4 H   embracing the challenge of doing business in a sustainable way
5 B   taking responsibility for your environment
6 A   playing a part in fighting poverty, unemployment and social injustice
7 C   being committed to growing your business by ethical means
8 E   being prepared to disclose information

10   1 As   2 the   3 to   4 have   5 up   6 what

11

Adjective	Noun
accountable	accountability
sustainable	**sustainability**
unjust	injustice
poor	**poverty**
environmental	environment
committed	**commitment**
involved	**involvement**
respectful (or **respected**)	respect
beneficial	benefit
honest	**honesty**
considerate	consideration

12   The general rule for words of three syllables or more is that the stress falls on the third syllable from the end, except:
with nouns that end -*tion*, and adjectives that end -*ic*, when the stress falls on the syllable before the final syllable;
with nouns that end -*ment*, where the stress falls in the same place as the verb they are derived from.

sustainable   sustainability
unjust   injustice
poor   poverty
environmental   environment
committed   commitment
involved   involvement
respectful   respect
beneficial   benefit
honest   honesty
considerate   consideration

8.2
Formal meetings

1   **Possible answers:**

1   What's on the agenda?
2   Could I just interrupt?
3   Sorry, could I just finish?
4   Can we move on?
5   I think we should take a break / adjourn for coffee.
6   Perhaps we can come back to this later.
7   That's a very good point.
8   We're running a little short of time.
9   I think John is better placed to answer that.
10   OK, let's leave it there. / I think we should stop there. To sum up, …

2   1   If I could just interrupt
2   could I just finish
3   That's a good point
4   we should move on to the next item on the agenda
5   I think Kate is better placed to answer that
6   If I understand you correctly

8.3
Reading Test: Part Four

1   1 C   2 A   3 A   4 D   5 D   6 B   7 C   8 B   9 B
10 D

MODULE 9
9.1
Innovation

1
1 Space Saving Kitchens	**neat and compact solutions**
2 Rioch Architects	**innovative state-of-the-art designs**
3 Presto Printing	**fast and efficient service**
4 TQ Clothing Company	**up-market designer labels at low prices**
5 Bettaprice Foods	**unbeatable value for money**
6 Durawork Power Tools	**reliable quality equipment**

2
1 compact	**bulky**
2 modern	**old-fashioned**
3 up-market	**down-market**
4 value for money	**overpriced**
5 reliable	**unreliable**
6 efficient	**inefficient**

3
/aɪ/	/ɪ/
private	equipment
finance	image
reliable	finish
realise	negative
client	limited
silent	efficient
	simple
	quality

4   1 at / in   2 of   3 in   4 at   5 to   6 on   7 with
8 with

5
at	in	on
the same time	the world	a small scale
home	the market*	the market*
the end of the day	the pipeline	holiday
least	the end	the face of it
	the future	average
	practice	

* *on the market* means 'available to buy', *in the market for* means you want to buy something.

6   **Possible answers:**
1   In principle, **that would be** no problem.
2   If you could deliver direct, **it would be** easier for us.
3   **I would accept** your invitation, but I'm afraid I have another appointment.
4   **I would appreciate** your help, because I don't think I can do it on my own.
5   If I were in your shoes, **I would do** the same.
6   Before agreeing anything, **we would need** certain guarantees from you.

7   1   Would you be prepared / willing to give us a discount?
2   I would need to discuss that with my boss.
3   That would be convenient for us too.
4   That would be difficult for us.
5   We would be happy to accept those terms.
6   In exchange, would you be able to guarantee that …

8   1   out of   2   up with   3   out for
4   up with   5   forward to   6   up to

9 1 The *competition* is general (=*all the competitors together*), a *competitor* is single and specific.

2 *Differentiate* is to make something be or appear different; *make a difference* is to make a contribution or have a noticeable effect

3 *Efficiency* is to do with saving time, money and effort; *effectiveness* is getting results.

4 When you are behind you have to *catch up* (*reach the same level*), then you have to *keep up* (=*stay at the same level*); finally, you *get ahead of the competition.*

5 You try to *retain* good employees (=*keep hold of*); you try to *sustain* an advantage (=*keep up*).

6 A *patent* gives the copyright or intellectual ownership of an idea; a *licence* is a permission to do or sell something.

10 1 innovative 2 followers 3 growth
4 spending 5 failures 6 driver
7 existing

9.2
Negotiating

1 1 True (*you have to treat the negotiation like a game ... if you lose, it's not the end of the world.*)

2 Doesn't say

3 False (*Your counterpart will see how much importance you have attached to getting the thing in question and will extract the highest price possible*)

4 Doesn't say

5 True (*Caring too much ... will make you lose your cool ... you also lose ... any natural shield ... against emotional manipulation by the other party*)

2 1 D 2 H 3 B 4 G 5 C 6 A 7 F 8 E

3 1 F 2 H 3 C 4 G 5 D 6 E 7 A

9.3
Reading and Listening Tests: Part Three

1 1 B *a seismic change*

2 D *completely redesign our cities and transport networks to be cleaner, quieter and less congested*

3 C *Even though there will have to be investments in new power generation capacity to supply the electricity needed to run the vehicles, these are likely to be greener power plants than those constructed in the past.*

4 A *traffic will flow freely without the need for controls ... reduce overall car ownership*

5 D *we will be able to arrange car trips in a way that is more convenient for all of us ... without any of the hassle ...*

6 C *China's central planning system ... avoids having different companies compete to own the winning technology*

MODULE 10
10.1
Travel and entertainment

1 1 Harvey 2 Amy 3 both 4 Harvey 5 Harvey
6 Harvey 7 both 8 Amy

2 A Ummmm ... I think I'll have the steak.
   A is looking at the menu and deciding now (spontaneous decision)

B I'm going to have the lobster.
   B has looked at the menu and already decided (plan or intention)

C I'm just having some soup.
   C has already ordered soup and is now waiting for it to arrive (arrangement)

3 *The present simple is used for schedules and timetables.*
The present continuous is used for arrangements.
'Going to' is used for things decided and also for confident predictions.
'Will' is used for general predictions, spontaneous decisions or offers and simple statement of fact.

1 is
2 are meeting
3 are you going to say
4 am going to tell / will tell
5 gives
6 will have / are going to have to
7 won't like / is not going to like
8 is happening
9 are hosting
10 will be / is going to be
11 will be / are
12 does / will it end
13 will bring / is bringing
14 am going to try

4 1
1 publicity 2 venue 3 reflect
4 put on 5 presentation
2
1 get 2 ice 3 treat
4 estimate 5 turn up

5 **go** missing / crazy / bankrupt / to plan / over budget / quiet / shopping
get to know someone / married / lost / tired / people involved / started

6 **Possible answers:**

I need to **get ready** for the meeting. It starts in five minutes.

She's a really nice woman when you **get to know** her.

A lot of things could **go wrong** if we don't prepare carefully.

He **got married** when he was 21.

I can't find the quotation I sent them. It's **gone missing**.

I'd take a taxi if I were you. It's very easy to **get lost** in the one way system.

She's **going to go crazy** when she finds out.

I am **getting** very **tired** of waiting.

They **went bankrupt** because of cashflow problems.

I always try to **get people involved** when I give a talk by giving them a little exercise to do.

If everything **goes to plan** the event should be a great success.

OK. Everyone's here. Shall we **get started**?

We **went** a little **over budget** but not too badly.

Are the launch preparations going OK? Things have **gone** very **quiet**.

I am going to **go shopping** at lunchtime.

7 1 The⌣y⌣ opening will be⌣y⌣a⌣teigh⌣tam.
2 We didn't go⌣w⌣ou⌣to⌣w⌣a restaurant.
3 I⌣y⌣a⌣minterested, if you⌣w⌣are.
4 Can we just go⌣w⌣over the⌣y⌣agenda?
5 Do you⌣w⌣ever lie⌣y⌣about you⌣rage?

10.2
The language of proposals

1 I would like to draw your attention <u>to the performance</u>
Unfortunately, <u>it has experienced some problems in the market</u>,
The <u>main problem is our advertising campaign</u>, not the product. We <u>need to find a different way to advertise the product</u>
By contrast, <u>they have used innovative styles of marketing and advertising</u>,
we should <u>design some advertisements which feel fresh and attractive</u> and run these on different types of advertising media: TV, radio, social media, billboards etc.
we <u>should use some famous people in the advertisements</u>, because this will help to persuade consumers that it is a good product

2 **Possible answer:**

To: The directors

Following the disappointing recent performance of the energy drink Zap, I would like to suggest some action we can take to reverse this trend.

Unfortunately, **sales have not grown at all in the last nine months**, while our competitors' products have improved their sales by an average of 8%. We need to take steps urgently to deal with this situation.

The main problem is our advertising campaign. **We are still running the original TV advertisement, using the same characters – a number of ordinary people, in their 30s mainly, doing various sports (with the help of Zap). We need to build a new story around the product, using new characters – perhaps well-known athletes** – to advertise the product or it will continue to lose market share to its competitors.

By contrast, our competitors have focused on the youth market by sponsoring events such as the World Skateboard championships. They have also placed their energy drinks in more specialised shops, like cycling shops. In this way, they have attracted a lot of new customers. We must do the same.

My recommendations are as follows:

– to employ some advertising specialists to help us define a new campaign.

– to create advertisements which appeal to a younger age group and use more humour. These could be run on TV and also on social media where young people are more likely to see them.

– to get the endorsement of an up-and-coming sporting hero, a footballer for example, that young people can really identify with.

Please consider these proposals carefully and do not hesitate to contact me for further details.

10.3
Speaking Test: Part Three

1 **Possible answers:**
- More use of video and telephone conferencing
- Travel only to essential meetings
- Try to stay for shorter periods when abroad
- Offer a prize for staff who save the most on travel

2 **Possible answers:**
1 What do you think about … / Do you have any views on …
2 In my opinion / For me
3 The main thing / The most important issue
4 On the other hand
5 I agree with you.
6 It is also true
7 furthermore / in addition
8 Good idea.
9 just to sum up
10 've agreed

MODULE 11

11.1

The economy

1 HC wanted to increase tax on the rich and on big companies; DT wanted to reduce taxes.

HC wanted to help the middle class; DT wanted to help the working class.

HC wanted hard work to be rewarded; DT wanted to create jobs by bringing manufacturing jobs back to America from overseas.

HC (The text doesn't say what her view on trade was); DT said he wanted trade deals that were more favourable for America.

2
1 cost of / standard of / ~~quality of~~ **living**
2 ~~blooming~~ / booming / buoyant **economy**
3 private / ~~civil~~ / public **sector**
4 job / labour / ~~work~~ **market**
5 **trade** ~~excess~~ / deficit / surplus
6 **tax** burden / bill / ~~load~~
7 **consumer** ~~faith~~ / confidence / spending
8 **government** ~~present~~ / subsidy / grant
9 **power** ~~consuming~~ / buying / purchasing

3 1 A 2 D 3 G 4 B 5 F 6 E

4
1 D relocate   2 B encourage
3 H depressed   4 I disabled
5 C competition   6 A confidence
7 G inefficiency   8 E unemployment

5
1 don't mind, will leave   2 was / were, would do
3 won't, is   4 would find, was / were not
5 wanted, would triple   6 would take, thought
7 will mind, borrow*

** If it was an unlikely request it would also be possible to say: 'Do you think that he **would mind** if I **borrowed** his car?'*

6 **Possible answers:**
1 if I had something very important that I needed to finish
2 if it were only a small gift
3 if the job involved a lot more stress and much longer hours
4 if I had enough money already to live out my retirement comfortably
5 if I felt I was not being taken seriously
6 if someone had made a really bad factual mistake

7 **Possible answers:**
1 More working mothers will stay in employment.
2 Unemployed people will be forced to find work.
3 A lot of high earners will leave the country.
4 It will encourage people to set up their own companies.

5 It will help children to learn key computer skills.
6 It will reduce the number of cars on the road.

8 **Long**: laid, f**oo**d, sleep, medium, incl**u**de, m**o**ve, range, client, b**o**th
Short: slip, s**ai**d, g**oo**d, ab**o**ve, m**e**dical, p**u**dding, cl**o**th, rang, clinic

10
1 outgoing   2 premises   3 rental
4 grants   5 estate   6 property
7 move   8 exempt

11 1 A 2 E 3 B 4 H 5 D 6 I 7 C 8 F

12 1 on 2 in 3 for 4 to 5 out 6 about
7 out, for 8 in 9 on

11.2

Effective writing

1
1 First of all
2 Moreover
3 Unfortunately
4 As we see it
5 For example
6 Indeed
7 To sum up
8 although

2 **Possible answers:**
1 We consider that $150 is too expensive for a top of the range hairdryer.
2 To sum up, my preference would be the second option, since it is important to find a more cost-effective solution.

3 **Possible answers:**
Dear Jim
I hope you are well. (**0**) I'm sorry about the long delay in replying to your email, (**1**) **but** I wanted to research your question thoroughly before (**2**) **replying.**
You (**3**) **asked if** it was possible to extend the life of our standard mobile phone battery, (**4**) **because** you have received a (**5**) **lot** of complaints about it. The answer is 'yes', but the solution may be expensive. We source our batteries from a Korean supplier which manufactures three different grades of battery. The ones (**6**) **we buy** are the cheapest in the range. (**7**) **Not surprisingly**, they also have the shortest life.
If you (**8**) **want** me to send you more technical details, (**9**) **feel free to** ask me.

11.3
Speaking Test: Part Two

1
1 find
2 making
3 have
4 on
5 easy
6 I have mentioned
7 to prioritise
8 would like to
9 make
10 to do
11 should
12 to
13 you can even have

2 Possible answers:
- In what kind of jobs is it important to be able to manage your time?
- With modern communications, is it easier or more difficult for business people to manage their time nowadays?

MODULE 12

12.1
Crossing cultures

1 Possible answers:
1 *global* village
2 multinational *corporations*
3 *trade* barriers
4 cheap *imports / goods*
5 *free* movement of capital
6 global *economy / market / trade*
7 *developed/ developing / under-developed* countries
8 deregulated *market / economy*

2
1 John J Sweeney
2 Robert J Samuelson
3 William Greider
4 Jack Welch
5 Fredric Jameson
6 Robert Reich

3
wish + past perfect
should + *have* + past participle
If + past perfect, *would* + *have* + past participle
could / might + *have* + past participle

Possible answers:
I **wish** they **hadn't sold** the business.
We **should have researched** the market more thoroughly.
If she **hadn't attended** the conference, she **wouldn't have missed** the deadline.
I **might have changed** my mind if I had read the report.

4
It must have been ...	99% yes
It might have been ...	50%
It may have been ...	50%
It could have been ...	50%
It can't have been ...	99% no

(*Could* is sometimes used for situations which seem less likely than *might* and *may*.)

5
1 If I **had felt** more confident, I would have taken the risk.
2 You should **have asked** me. I would have said 'yes'.
3 If you had lost it, I **would have been** furious.
4 I wish that I **hadn't mentioned** that I was looking for another job.
5 I don't know why he's so late. I suppose he might **have forgotten**.
6 I don't think anyone could **have predicted** that this would happen.

6
1 They wished they had done more tests before launching the new product.
2 They could have got a better response if they had advertised externally.
3 He should have consulted more people.
4 She wished that she had gone to university.
5 If she had kept her shares, she would have lost a lot of money.
6 If either side had made a compromise, they might have reached an agreement.
7 I should have taken the job.
8 They could have avoided bankruptcy if they had invested more.

7 Normally a 'g' is hard if followed by the vowels *a*, *o*, *u* and soft if followed by *e* or *i*. But there are exceptions!
Hard: target, colleague, angle, guest, legal, global
Soft: merge, manager, gentleman, angel, gesture, region, margin

8
1 casually OR formally
2 shake hands OR nod your head
3 by his / her formal title OR by his / her first name
4 exchanging small talk OR chatting OR getting to know him / her

9 The ultimate gesture = the smile

10
1 nod	2 common	3 contact
4 feature	5 losing	6 rude
7 greet	8 hand	9 Awareness

12.2
Social English

1 1 H 2 D 3 I 4 F 5 G 6 C 7 E 8 A

2 Possible answers:

   1 Pleased to meet you, Jane.

   2 Don't worry. I'm not in a hurry.

   3 Not at all. / You're very welcome.

   4 Yes, it is.

   5 Not bad, thanks.

   6 That's very kind of you, but I can manage.

   7 Thank you. So are you.

   8 That would be great.

   9 Please. Go ahead.

  10 No, go ahead / Actually, I'd rather you didn't.

3 1 well   2 to hear   3 would be   4 out   5 worry
6 go ahead   7 in   8 so   9 it   10 of

12.3
Reading Test: Part Five and Part Six

1 1 its   2 of   3 even   4 with   5 not   6 had   7 was
8 than   9 at   10 then

2
1 Correct	2 can	3 Correct
4 with	5 not	6 Correct
7 more	8 Correct	9 on
10 been	11 Correct	12 that